洪觀 時代 TRANSFORMING VISIONS

洪建全基金會 50 年
HONG FOUNDATION 50 YEARS

目錄
INDEX

50TH

以文化傳家

我自 1969 年從美國學成歸國，進入洪家的事業經營，我的學思背景及對社會的關懷，促成洪建全教育文化基金會的創立。從此我開始跨足在企業界與文化界之間，過起忙碌豐富又快樂的人生，真是感恩！

五十年來基金會的行事，大都是以文化引導的觀念，播下文化與教育的種籽。階段性的目標任務也都在一一達成後再轉化提升。在當時的台灣開風氣之先，也為洪家創造以「文化」傳家的形象！

每一次的轉化提升，多年後看來都是在「必要的情況」下發生，而每一個過程卻都是充滿期盼興奮，有時也是痛苦的抉擇。感謝一路走來幫助提攜的長輩、朋友和同事，我們一起走過意義非凡的路程！

簡靜惠

洪建全基金會榮譽董事長

MESSAGE FROM THE HONORARY CHAIRMAN

Cultivating Culture Across Generations

I began working for the Hong family business after returning to Taiwan following my studies in the United States in 1969. My academic background and interest in social outreach drove my active involvement in the creation of the Hong Foundation. Since then, my career straddling the worlds of business and culture has, while being exceedingly busy, been highly rewarding and satisfying. For this, I am eternally grateful!

For the past half century, the foundation, guided by the ideas and ideals of culture, has been dedicated to sowing the seeds of culture and education. The progressive attainment of its goals has dynamically transformed and improved the foundation through these many years. Also, the nurturing openness of contemporary Taiwan society was crucial in helping secure the Hong family's legacy as a leading patron of culture and the arts.

Every transformative turn in the foundation's path was, in retrospect, made in response to some new and significant ripple in the larger social landscape. Moreover, although some of our changes weren't easy, every shift in direction was greeted with expectation and excitement. I wish to thank all of those who have supported our endeavors as well as my friends and colleagues, both past and present. Our journey together has been truly remarkable!

Celia Hong Chien Chinghui

Honorary Chairman, Hong Foundation

董事長的話

文化創造產業

美國的開國元老之一、第二任總統約翰·亞當斯（John Adams）曾寫道：「我必須修習政治學與戰爭學，我們的後代才能在民主之上修習數學、哲學；我們的後代必須修習數學、哲學、地理學、博物學、航海學、商業和農業，他們的後代才能在科學之上學習繪畫、詩歌、音樂、建築、雕刻等人文藝術。」

二次戰後，台灣社會漸趨穩定，我的祖父洪建全先生有幸在經濟開始發展之際，投身貿易與製造業，並在商業上取得成就。但不滿足於個人事業的成功，洪建全先生很有遠見地將注意力轉向藝術、文學、音樂，認為文化教育的培養將會成為台灣下一階段社會發展的動能，因此成立「洪建全教育文化基金會」。

「技術採用生命週期」（Technology Adoption Life Cycle）是高科技業很熟悉的概念，描繪著任何一個創新科技產品被市場採納的過程。在這個模型中，最先採納創新產品的是少數「創新者」（innovators），接下來是「早期採用者」（early adopters），然後是「早期大眾」（early majority）和市場飽和後的「晚期大眾」（late majority），最後是「落伍者」（laggards）。手機就是一個經典的案例可以說明這個模式。譬如傳統手機已經到了「落伍者」階段，而智慧型手機在 2017 年出貨量達到高峰後，已逐年下滑，開始進入「晚期大眾」階段。當然不是每樣新科技都能順利依序滲透市場，任何創新產品

及其進入大眾主流所遇到最主要的挑戰是成功跨越「創新者」的鴻溝並移動到「早期採用者」。

我認為這個模式也可以應用在所謂文化基因（meme）的傳遞上。「文化基因」是 1976 年由世界知名的科學作家、演化生物學家理查·道金斯（Richard Dawkins）所提出，代表人與人之間文化傳遞的基本單位。像 DNA 裡的基因一樣，人類可以透過寫作、說話、手勢、儀式，或是其他可以複製或模仿的現象，將文化基因傳遞給其他人。我們若用文化的角度套用上述的生命週期：「前衛思想」的概念藝術、實驗性劇場、地下音樂等可被視為「創新者」；「另類文化」的小劇場、當代藝術、另類音樂等可以對應到「早期採用者」；「次文化」如設計師、建築師等介於「早期採用者」與「早期大眾」間；而「大眾文化」如流行音樂、好萊塢電影、通俗藝術等則從「早期大眾」延伸到「晚期大眾」和「落伍者」。美國藝術家 Ryan McGinness 的作品上寫著：「Everything you like I liked 5 years ago（你現在喜歡的一切，我五年前喜歡過了）」——這句話說出了重點。就像流行音樂的發展一樣，五年前的地下獨立音樂，現在在熱門歌曲的排行榜上；這在電影、表演藝術、劇場和熱門文化上也有相同的現象。

我一直認為「文創產業」這個被大肆推廣的概念本身是自相矛盾的。藝術創作核心在於獨特的表現方式與觀

點，和量產的商業行為牴觸；另一方面，從商業的角度來看，要靠文化藝術賺取可觀的利潤回報是極度困難且不實際的。如果企圖討好大眾市場，產出的作品就會失去實驗精神和藝術意義。

過去五十年，洪建全基金會一直扮演的角色就是文化領域的開拓者，以非營利、實驗精神和多元化的發展模式，支持和贊助那些尚屬於極少數「創新者」或「早期採用者」的創作與藝文活動。一旦這些創作跨越鴻溝、被大眾接受及獲取成功後，基金會就完成階段性任務。例如在雲門舞集成立之初、民歌尚在萌芽階段，基金會早已支持贊助，等到民歌蔚為風潮、市場反應熱烈，就退場。「文經學苑」亦是如此。在 80 年代的台灣社會，願意投資企業領導人學習人文素養的人寥寥可數。等到社會大眾逐漸熟悉並開始出現類似教育課程，基金會就另啟新的項目。

我父親洪敏隆先生在三十年前創立「文經學苑」時曾寫過一篇文章〈雲和石〉，內容提到：「雲在天上的飄渺、變化、美麗，有如理想一般的遙不可及。石在地上的實在、堅硬、冷酷，有如現實一般的不可避免。把雲和石，比喻為文化與經濟，是我的一種想法，也是一種期待，期待在經濟帶動社會繁榮的同時，也能留意到人們的生活品質。二者，有時會衝突，有時也會遙遠不可及，但是，雲彩有雲彩的美，石頭有石頭的可愛，如

何將兩者結合，其主力在人。」

近年來我經常思考文化和產業的共存關係。不是產業創造文化，恰恰相反地，是文化孕育產業。這個概念與我父親在〈雲和石〉的想法同步一致。我相信「文化創造產業」，而人文和藝術是啟發和推動未來產業的關鍵。因此我們的目光不能在短期價值的追尋，而是要著眼於能夠對社會產生深遠和正面影響的價值，而這些價值將長期為產業創造新的視野。

在過去的五十年，基金會走在時代的前端，不斷地向前展望。我特別感謝我的母親簡靜惠女士，從首任執行長、董事長，到現在身為基金會的榮譽董事長，她五十年來的領導和指引，為基金會灌溉了不斷創新的精神及新穎大膽的想法和開明態度。銘記我父親對「雲與石」的想法，並在基金會大膽求新求變的基因延續下，我堅信能將基金會的精神發揚光大。

展望未來五十年，基金會將堅持並進一步發展我們的創始使命，即發展文化教育作為下一階段社會發展的動能。我們將繼續推動和支持前衛的思想與創作，期待能創造新的思潮與典範，在社會中扎根、萌芽和擴散，最終為產業創造新的機遇和活力。我們的使命是：滋養一個「讓前衛文化進展的力量滲透到產業及社會中」的環境；讓創作成為企業、產業和社會的養分和動力。

洪建全基金會董事長
台灣松下電器董事長

MESSAGE FROM THE CHAIRMAN

Culture Creates Industry

The Founding Father and the second President of the United States John Adams once wrote, "I must study politics and war, that our sons may have liberty to study mathematics and philosophy. Our sons ought to study mathematics and philosophy, geography, natural history and naval architecture, navigation, commerce and agriculture in order to give their children a right to study painting, poetry, music, architecture, statuary, (and other pursuits in the arts and humanities)."

As Taiwan society was settling back into normalcy following the Second World War and the national economy stood at the cusp of making its robust turnaround, my grandfather Hong Chienchuan (C.C.) (洪建全) had the good fortune of achieving remarkable success in international trade and manufacturing. Not content to sit on his laurels, he turned his attention to the arts, literature and music, with the foresight of fostering education of culture as a means to fuel the next phase of social development in Taiwan. To this end, he founded the Hong Foundation (洪建全教育文化基金會).

The technology adoption life cycle, a concept well known in the high-tech sector, describes how markets typically adopt innovative technologies. Under this model, any product innovation would initially be embraced by a relatively small number of "innovators," followed by the "early adopters" then the "early majority." Only after market saturation are these products accepted by the "late majority" and lastly, by the "laggards." Mobile phones are one such product example that illustrates the technology adoption life cycle. The basic cell phone is now clearly at the "laggards" end of the curve, while smartphones, sales of which peaked in 2017, are now moving downwards on the "late majority" section of the adoption curve. Of course, not all technological

innovations meet with commercial success. The main challenge for any innovation, and for it to enter the mainstream, is to make the successful leap from "innovators" to "early adopters" on the adoption curve.

I think the adoption life cycle model is also applicable to the transmission of cultural "memes." The term "meme" was first coined by renowned science author and evolutionary biologist Richard Dawkins in 1976 to represent the basic unit or idea of culture. Similar to DNA, memes are transmitted between people through various replicable, imitable medium such as writing, speech, gestures and rituals. If we frame the technology adoption life cycle in the context of culture, then avant-garde art, experimental theater and underground music may be considered the "innovators" on the adoption curve. Following this thread, alternative and various sub-genres of contemporary art, theater and music would be "early adopters;" design and architecture would be somewhere between "early adopters" and "early majority" and mainstream culture such as pop music, Hollywood movies and pop art would occupy the wide swath from "early majority" through to "late majority" and "laggards." When American artist Ryan McGinness wrote, "Everything you like I liked 5 years ago," he was absolutely spot on in expressing this cultural pattern. In many instances, underground music of five years ago is now the hottest music on the charts today. This holds true across different art forms -be it film, performance art, theater or pop culture.

I believe the widely promoted "cultural and creative industries" (「文創產業」) mandate to be self-contradictory. Mass commercialism is antithetical to the expression of a unique and singular vision which is crucial to artistic creativity. On the other hand, for businesses to project sizable profit returns from the arts is exceedingly difficult and unrealistic. Art created to please the masses predictably lacks both experimental spirit and artistic meaning.

For the past 50 years, the Hong Foundation has been a pioneer in supporting and funding creative "innovators" and "early adopters," with a mindset that is not-for-profit, experimental, and diverse. Once their creative work makes the transition to wider public acceptance and success, the foundation's work there is done. The Hong Foundation was instrumental in supporting both Cloud Gate Theater (雲門舞集) and Taiwan's folk music scene during their earliest, formative years; after they gained market traction and popularity, the foundation phased out its active involvement. The Culture For Business Academy (文經學苑) followed a similar course. In the 80s, few if any, were invested in the study of humanities for business leaders in Taiwan. When public awareness grew and similar education programs emerged, the foundation then discontinued the academy and began other projects.

My father Hong Minlong (M.L.) (洪敏隆) wrote an essay entitled "Cloud and Stone" (雲和石) three decades ago at the founding of the Culture For Business Academy. In it, he wrote, "Clouds float freely in the sky; ever changing, ever beautiful. Like lofty ideals, they remain distant and beyond reach. Stones on the ground are tangible, solid and indifferent. Like the trials and tribulations of everyday life, they are inevitable. Using clouds and stones respectively as metaphors for culture and industry encapsulates for me both an idea and a vision. It is my hope that as economic growth brings prosperity, it also raises the quality of life for society at large. Clouds and stones exist on their own terms and, just as culture and industry, their qualities are conflicting and seemingly mutually exclusive. How to unite them in harmony is for us to endeavor."

For the past few years, I've often considered the symbiosis between culture and industries. Instead of industries giving rise to culture. I believe the contrary, it is actually culture that births industries. This idea is in sync with my father's thoughts elucidated in "Cloud and Stone." I believe "Culture Creates Industry," and that both humanities and the arts are critical in inspiring and driving future industries. Therefore we must set our sights not on short-term values but on values that can deeply and positively impact society, values that will create new horizons for industries in the long term.

For the past half century, the Hong Foundation has been at the forefront of its times, looking always toward the future. I wish to express my deepest gratitude to the Honorary Chairman of the Hong Foundation, my mother Celia Hong Chien Chinghui (簡靜惠). Her leadership and guidance over the past fifty years have instilled in the foundation its spirit of ceaseless innovation and openness for new and bold ideas. With my father's thoughts on "Cloud and Stone" within me, and empowered by the foundation's DNA, I stand with conviction to carry the foundation's legacy forward.

Looking 50 years ahead, the foundation will uphold and evolve further our founding mission of fostering education of culture as a means to fuel the next phase of social development. We will continue to incubate and support pioneering ideas and creativity so that new thought paradigms may germinate, take hold and diffuse throughout society, to ultimately create new horizons of opportunity and energize growth for industries. This is our mission: to nurture an ecosystem of creators by fostering an environment where the power of disruptive creativity can permeate society to become nutrients for future industries.

Royce YC Hong

Chairman, Hong Foundation
Chairman, Panasonic Taiwan

副董事長的話

持續求變求新的典範傳承

洪建全基金會五十年來對教育和文化的支持，既是一個家族的精神財富，也等同於台灣社會文化的資產。

1953 年，礦工之子洪建全先生創立了「國際牌」這個家電品牌，1962 年，洪建全與松下幸之助合資成立「台灣松下電器股份有限公司」。在台灣還處於戒嚴時期的 1971 年，洪先生很有遠見地成立「洪建全教育文化基金會」，致力於提倡教育和文化。

70 年代，洪建全基金會以《書評書目》雜誌開啟了文學評論的先聲；並首開當時台灣新局，以台灣收藏最豐的音樂黑膠唱片和電影資料，帶起了台灣民俗音樂的復興；在台灣經濟成長指數激增的 80 年代，基金會以「文經學苑」開創了人文與企業合一的先河；90 年代以「敏隆講堂」為名設立的現代學堂，人人在此學習文史哲藝課程與深度閱讀；到了 2000 年後期，透過委託及直接贊助，支持跨越各學科領域、當代藝術家的「覓計畫」，正式啟動。

在基金會多元經營又不斷開展的精神裡，始終有個核心價值是：藉著支持當代創作者來激發「創作文化」；創作者以作品來表達他們持續求新求變的典範。過去五十年來，基金會影響了各領域的作家、表演藝術家、音樂家、電影製片人、國際級知名的編舞家……如雲門舞集創辦人林懷民和電影導演李安等才華橫溢的藝術家。

為了慶祝及紀念洪建全基金會五十年前所開啟的這段令人難以置信又驚艷的絕妙旅程，我們以這本《洪觀時代》影像書呈現給我們的家人、朋友、終生支持者和廣大的合作者；還有這五十年來，沿途不斷加入基金會的所有朋友；我們的內心無比歡喜，又領受著無上榮耀；來自你們的慷慨和莫大的信任，我們將永銘於心，無日或忘。是您們共同的參與和創造，形塑了今日的我們。

這些無價、珍貴的歷史照片檔案，不僅僅是令人驚歎的視覺紀錄，還真實呈現了洪建全基金會映照著當下時代精神所展現出來兼具廣度和深度的視野。在展望下一個五十年之際，我們將懷抱著謙卑和感恩之心，傳承洪建全基金會的精神資產，傾盡全力為下一代經營出比好還要更好的基金會。

張淑征

洪建全基金會副董事長暨執行長
十一事務所共同創辦人暨主持建築師

MESSAGE FROM THE VICE CHAIRMAN

A Legacy of Shifting Paradigms

The Hong Foundation's five decades support to education and culture is a family legacy that is synonymous with the social cultural heritage of Taiwan.

In 1953, Hong Chienchuan (C.C.) (洪建全), the son of a miner, founded "Guojipai" (國際牌), the legendary home appliances brand which later became Panasonic Taiwan (台灣松下電器). In 1971, he established the Hong Foundation to advocate education and culture when Taiwan was still under martial law.

Throughout the 70s, the Hong Foundation spawn the birth of literary criticism with the *Shu Ping Shu Mu* (書評書目) *Review of Books and Bibliography* publication; and brought on the Taiwanese folk music revival with trail-blazing vinyl compilations from its music and movie collection which was the largest of such in Taiwan then. During the exponential economic rise of Taiwan in the 80s, the Hong Foundation pioneered the integrated studies of humanities and entrepreneurship with the Culture For Business Academy (文經學苑). The 90s saw Minlong Forum's (敏隆講堂) extensive dissemination of humanities education and reading cultures for adults. In late 2000s, Project Seek (覓計畫) was launched to support a range of interdisciplinary, contemporary artists through commissions and direct sponsorships.

Underpinning the Hong Foundation's diverse and evolving patronage, there remains one central tenet of fostering the "Culture of Creation" by supporting an ecosystem of creators of their time; creators that were shifting paradigms through their work at the time. Over the last 50 years, the Hong Foundation has influenced numerous writers, performance artists, musicians, film makers, artists of caliber in the ranks of internationally renown choreographer and dancer Lin Hwaimin (林懷民) of Cloud Gate Theatre (雲門舞集) and director Ang Lee (李安).

To commemorate this incredible journey that we've embarked on 50 years ago, and where we've arrived at today, it is our pleasure and great honor to present this photo book *Transforming Visions* to our family, friends, life-long supporters, our vast community of collaborators and to all who have joined the Hong Foundation along the way. We are forever beholden to your generosity and immense trust. We are also shaped by your collective creativity.

These priceless historical photographs and archival records not only serve as a stunning visual record, they truly capture the breadth and depth of the vision of the Hong Foundation, seen against the spirit of its time. As we look forward to our next 50 years, we carry the legacy of the Hong Foundation with humility and gratitude, and will endeavor to build it even better for the next generation.

Grace Cheung

Vice Chairman & Executive Director, Hong Foundation
Co-Founder & Principal Architect, XRANGE Architecture + Design

時代見證

齊邦媛

作家·現年 98 歲

————

簡靜惠以歷史畢業生的理想，設置敏隆講堂發揮現代人文休憩站的功能，在這個紛亂、災難頻襲的時代，人們最需要強韌的內心力量……她投入文化講座和活動深廣的影響，都已深植在台灣社會進展的歷史裡。

許倬雲

歷史學家·現年 92 歲

————

敏隆講堂掀起台灣社會的民間講學風氣，也激發一股人文學習的風潮……並逐步擴大為有系統的開辦文史哲藝課程，致力於提倡人文素養及文化關懷，這是為台灣厚培文化土壤……

黃春明

作家

————

洪建全基金會一直有很好的表現，在閱讀風氣消失的今天，面對出版社一直關掉，重慶南路的書店也只剩下幾家，大家都忙著滑手機，敏隆講堂的人文課程能長期堅持，彌足珍貴。

FIVE DECADES OF REFLECTIONS

Chi Pangyuan

Author (98 years old this year)

———

In creating Minlong Forum as an oasis for the humanities and humanistic studies, Celia Hong Chien Chinghui put her academic background in history to exceptional use. In today's troubled and disaster-prone times, we all will do well to work on tempering our intrinsic fortitude. Celia's cultural courses and activities have had a wide-ranging and positive impact, and have become an enduring part of social development in Taiwan.

Hsu Choyun

Historian (92 years old this year)

———

Minlong Forum provided critical inspiration for both the grassroots community education movement and the resurgence of interest in humanities-related studies in Taiwan. This forum later expanded, offering full curricula in literature, history, philosophy and the arts, with a faculty dedicated to cultivating in their students' humanistic values and cultural sensitivity. Minlong Forum is truly fertile soil in which to foster cultural progress in Taiwan.

Hwang Chunming

Author

———

The Hong Foundation has been an emphatically positive and abiding presence in society. Today, with reading for pleasure at an all-time low, well-established publishing houses foundering and failing, just a handful of bookshops still operating in Taipei's once-thriving bookseller district, and smartphones claiming much of the public's attention, the Hong Foundation's continued sponsorship of humanities courses at Minlong Forum is precious indeed.

林懷民

雲門舞集創辦人／創團藝術總監

———

當年（1974 年）因為您（簡靜惠）的慷慨，支援雲門做這個事（贊助賴德和的作品《白蛇傳》），音樂家因此能夠發表他們的作品，廣大的群眾也認識了李泰祥、許博允、賴德和、溫隆信，馬水龍這幾位年輕的本土作曲家。台灣開始有了一個音樂的氛圍。那是一個很值得懷念的時代。

詹宏志

作家·PChome Online 董事長

———

基金會在每一個時期的創意與開展，都跟台灣社會文化發展有緊密相聯的邏輯，我也在不同階段受到不同的啟發，現在回頭看，彷彿基金會和我人生一直相伴。

楊照

作家·新匯流基金會董事長

———

在台灣文學史上，《書評書目》最大特色在於包容性⋯⋯我會認為《書評書目》最容易、也最快速反應出時代的關心議題⋯⋯讀者也就很快的在書與評論間，找到嚴肅與認真的連結。

（摘自簡靜惠著《植栽一座文化森林—洪建全基金會 50 年》）

Lin Hwaimin

Founder, Cloud Gate Dance Theatre of Taiwan

––––––

That year (1974) because of your (Chien Chinghui) generosity, you supported Cloud Gate to do this (sponsoring Lai Deho's work *The Legend of the White Snake*), so musicians were able to publish their works, and the general public also got to know Lee Taihsiang, Hsu Poyun, David Wen Loonghsing, Lai Deho, Ma Shuilong these few young local composers. Taiwan began to have a musical atmosphere. It was an era worth remembering.

Jan Hungtze

Author, Chairman of PChome Online Inc.

––––––

The Hong Foundation has always aligned its creativity and efforts closely with domestic social development trends here in Taiwan. In thinking back on the various inspired ideas I've had over my career, I cannot help but notice the close and formative influence that the foundation has had on me nearly every step of the way.

Yang Chao

Author, Chairman of Hyper Convergence Foundation

––––––

The uniqueness in Taiwan literary history of the magazine *Shu Ping Shu Mu Review of Books and Bibliography* lies in its inclusiveness. I believe reading *Shu Ping Shu Mu* was the easiest and fastest way to grasp the key issues and concerns of the day. Readers of this magazine also tapped into the most serious and earnest connection between books and related critical analysis.

(excerpted from *Planting a Forest of Culture - The First 50 Years of the Hong Foundation* by Celia Hong Chien Chinghui)

世代觀點

吳明益

國立東華大學華文系教授

小時候中華商場的對面就是洪建全基金會，當時當然不可能知道它在做什麼。直到在東華大學任教時，當我們需要邀請國際上的華文作家來台灣演講，帶給台灣不同的文化交流時，洪建全基金會的敏隆講堂、銅鐘經典講座就伸出援手。這就像童年時遙遠的，想像和文化並無太深聯繫的一個知名品牌，在我們推廣文學時備感艱難時給予我們最可貴的、實質的協助，我們感動並且感謝這樣的文化實踐。也希望基金會在台灣社會永遠存在。

———

林平

前台北市立美術館館長
東海大學美術系專任教授

1971 年迄今、五十年、半世紀是「洪建全基金會」的永續承諾，它不只來自於民間和創業家的原創精神，更從基金會營運的首日始，成為長久陪伴台灣社會提升人文素養、茁壯人才培育的鮮明標誌。從社會公益事業出發，不但吻合當代社會脈動，更具有時代前瞻精神；「洪建全基金會」超越了一個家族的所能，從經典到當代，跨越了多重價值門檻，彰顯了營運跨世代、受眾跨齡別、服務跨領域、視野跨世紀、持續更新前行的宏大職志！

郝廣才

格林文化發行人
格林文化事業股份有限公司社長

我永遠不會忘記，第一次踏進中華路「洪建全基金會」，在那裡看到卡拉揚指揮柏林愛樂的影片！我很像站在一個木箱，頭剛好超過圍牆，看見音樂可以神奇！可以偉大！

那兩個小時，點亮我的眼睛！只要想起來，我就能清楚看見我發亮的眼睛！

我相信台灣很多人跟我一樣，都曾被「洪建全基金會」點亮心中的火炬，照亮心中的夢想！

在那個到處都是牆的台灣，洪建全基金會是一個箱子，讓我們看過圍牆；是一面窗子，讓我們呼吸不一樣的空氣！在以前茫茫黃沙中，引進一泉活水；在當下滾滾洪流中，另闢一彎清溪。

CONTEMPORARY INSIGHTS

Wu Mingyi

Professor, Department of Sinophone Literature, National Dong Hwa University

I remember as a kid seeing the Hong Foundation's office across the street from Chunghwa Market in downtown Taipei. Of course, back then, I had no idea what the Hong Foundation was or what it did. This all changed after I started teaching at National Dong Hwa University and needed to invite overseas Sinophone writers to give lectures and promote related cultural exchange in Taiwan. The Hong Foundation's Minlong Forum and Tung Chung Master Lecture Series both generously stepped up to help me in this endeavor. This familiar yet enigmatic 'brand' from childhood, which I had not previously associated with cultural matters, lending us assistance at such a critical and difficult juncture in our literary promotion efforts was as fortuitous as it was effective. The Hong Foundation's good work in the advancement of culture is something that is both quite moving and truly appreciated. It is my sincere hope that the foundation remains forever woven into the fabric of Taiwan society.

———

Lin Ping

Former Director of the Taipei Fine Arts Museum
Professor, Department of Fine Arts, College of Fine Arts and Creative Design, Tunghai University

Its accomplishments over the past half century since its founding in 1971 testify to the sustainability of the Hong Foundation and its mission. The foundation is rooted not only in the innovative spirit of talented individuals and entrepreneurs but in its persistent cultivation of cultural literacy and individual talent across Taiwan society. As a charitable organization, the Hong Foundation's efforts have closely followed social trends while reflecting a progressive, forward-looking spirit. The contributions of the Hong Foundation exceed greatly what any one family could have accomplished on its own. From classic to contemporary, the foundation has successfully embraced multiple lanes of artistic and creative expression, crossing professional, age, and sectoral boundaries; sustaining its vision into a new century; and continuing to refine its mission into the future.

Hao Kuangtsai

Publisher and President of Grimm Press

I shall never forget my first visit to the Hong Foundation's office on Chunghua Road in downtown Taipei City. It was there that I saw for the first time Herbert von Karajan directing the Berlin Philharmonic Orchestra! I felt like a giddy child standing on a wooden crate craning his head just high enough to see over the wall and partake in this rivetingly glorious performance.

Those two short hours opened my eyes! Even now, I can still clearly remember how bright and doe-eyed I was that day.

I have no doubt there are many like me who have been deeply inspired and motivated by the Hong Foundation to find and pursue their passions.

In a society with a surfeit of 'walls', the Hong Foundation offers crates just high enough to stand on and see the potential that beckons on the other side. The foundation is a window through which refreshingly different breezes flow, a bubbling spring in an arid desert, and a clear, spring-fed pool created in a tumultuous maelstrom.

張鐵志

VERSE 雜誌創辦人暨總編輯

洪建全基金會五十年的故事就是一部台灣的跨界文化史，從音樂、出版、兒童文學，到思想講堂和當代藝術，他們用深耕與累積支持台灣文化前進，而下一個五十年會是更多的創新與實驗，重新想像台灣文化的可能。

———

彭俊亨

文化部前政務次長
元智大學文化產業與文化政策博士學程副教授

堅持五十年，洪建全基金會以人文的視野、素直的感懷、藝術的力量引領、驅動並回應社會的變遷與發展，也透過資源連結促進社會包容。安頓身心的講堂和空間，是匯集文史哲藝，激盪思辨和創造力的交流共學平台。欣見組織不斷地學習成長，超越、蛻變出獨特的經營風格，開創先趨，另樹一幟而斐然永續。當大家都在談 ESG、SDGs，基金會早在五十年前即揭示以「文化」做為永續發展的核心價值，落實踐行至今。未來 HAX 計畫奠基在使命傳承的路徑上與時俱進，展現創新前瞻，為所當為。在此致上老員工的深深期待與敬意。

蔡政憲

訊聯生物科技股份有限公司董事長

這本五十年紀念冊，見證了「洪建全基金會」在過去半世紀裡，戮力完成的台灣文化基因編輯的偉業，而我，也正是這時代中眾多接受此文化基因轉殖的其中一人。1982 年，我高二，沉迷西洋搖滾樂，因為文化上的沒自信，和大家一樣隨波逐流，沒想到卻在雲門舞集表演現場被陳達的音樂吸引住，像被雷打到的震撼，讓我隔天立即翹課衝去洪建全基金會說 :「我要陳達的音樂！」開開心心地把北管、南管等整套民樂買回家，與我心愛的搖滾樂團 Led Zeppelin、Pink Floyd 的唱片並列。一把月琴顛覆我的宇宙，啟發並從此改變我文化探索的範疇，開始大量蒐集傳統音樂戲曲、廟宇建築、民間慶典，影響直到今日。

不論是史惟亮、許常惠大量採集台灣民樂，不論是楊弦、李雙澤帶動起民歌，或是一群深深耕耘台灣攝影、茶文化的藝術家，多少具開拓性的創新，帶來深層而巨大的影響，也讓我更愛台灣！而這一切不是偶然，都是有像洪建全基金會這樣的有識之士，用文化改殖這半世紀以來的台灣。我多麼感謝基金會開啟的絕妙旅程，以及 Grace、Royce 兩位用心傳遞如文化聖火的志業，讓台灣這麼美！欣聞基金會創辦的台灣第一本書評雜誌《書評書目》近期將線上復刊，也非常期待五十年後的第二本紀念冊，記錄下個半世紀的恢弘視野。

Chang Tiehchih

Founder and Editor-in-Chief of VERSE

The Hong Foundation's first fifty years is the story of modern Taiwan's cross-cultural experience. The foundation has cultivated and steadily supported the advancement of Taiwan culture in a myriad of ways, covering music, publishing, children's literature, philosophical courses, and contemporary art. The Hong Foundation's next half century promises even more innovations and experimentation as the foundation helps reimagine and realize the rich potential of Taiwan culture.

———

Kevin Peng Chunheng

Former Deputy Minister, Ministry of Culture
Associate Professor, Ph.D Program in Cultural Industries and Cultural Policy, Yuan Ze University

For the past fifty years, the Hong Foundation has leveraged its cultured perspective, empathy, and artistic vigor to lead, stimulate, and embrace social trends and developments in Taiwan as well as linked resources together to promote social inclusiveness. The Hong Foundation's educational facilities and spaces for the promotion of mental and physical wellbeing are platforms for exchange and learning that bring together literature, history, philosophy and art to stimulate cognition and creativity. It has been my pleasure to see the foundation continually improve and mature, growing into its unique operational approach. It has blazed a pioneering trail that has made it truly exceptional. Although ESGs and SDGs are now all the rage, the foundation had already laid out why "culture" is so crucial to sustainable development 50 years ago, and incorporated this axiom into its operations ever since. At the heart of the coming HAX Program is the adaptation of the ongoing mission to the times, which was both progressive and practical. I, a former employee of the foundation, wish here to express my heartfelt anticipation and respect.

Chris Tsai

Chairman of BIONET Corp

This fifty year memorial book bears witness to the half century of good work done by the Hong Foundation to 'edit' the genes of Taiwan culture. I was one of the many beneficiaries of this genetic engineering enterprise. In 1982, I was an awkward high school student who, together with my peers, was a feckless fan of Western rock music. It was a total surprise then how much the music of Chen Da struck a chord in me at a Cloud Gate Theatre performance I attended. It was like I'd been struck by lightning! I skipped class the very next day and hurried over to the Hong Foundation's office. "I want to buy Chen Da's music!" I announced. I bought the entire set- both Beiguan and Nanguan music- and set them proudly alongside my Led Zeppelin and Pink Floyd albums. The traditional Chinese lute changed everything for me, changed completely my approach to cultural exploration. I began earnestly collecting traditional Taiwanese music and opera songs, delved into the intricacies of temple architecture, and investigated Taiwan's myriad folk festivals. The effects of this transformative experience remain with me even today.

The groundbreaking innovations and deep influence of Taiwan folk musicologists Shih Weiliang and Hsu Tsanghouei, progenitors of the Taiwanese folk music genre Yang Hsien and Lee Shuangtze, and the many artists who have dedicated their lives to Taiwanese photography and tea culture have made me love Taiwan all the more! But none of this has been by chance. Like the Hong Foundation, all of these individuals share deep, indelible ties to this land and each has had a transformative impact on Taiwan over the past half century. I am extremely grateful to the foundation for commencing this exquisite journey, and to Grace and Royce for their dedication to advancing a cultural renaissance that has made Taiwan so beautiful. I was pleased to hear that Taiwan's first book-review magazine *Shu Ping Shu Mu*, founded and published by the Hong Foundation, will soon be made available online. I am also looking very much forward to seeing the next Hong Foundation memorial book, highlighting the visionary ideas and accomplishments to come, published on the foundation's 100th anniversary.

劉若瑀

優人神鼓・財團法人優人文化藝術基金會創辦人
台北表演藝術中心董事長

洪家人總是，第一個發現如何將我們生活的環境和我們的成長連結！大學剛剛畢業，蘭陵劇坊演的那齣「新春歌謠音樂會」，是我人生聽到的第一個贊助表演藝術企業家的名字「洪建全」！多年後我成立了優人神鼓，那年優人受邀巴黎夏日藝術節演出，同時要在法國雲腳。我們邀請洪簡靜惠女士一起去。本以為她是去巴黎渡假，不會參加雲腳的部分，沒想到翻山越嶺整整五天的徒步雲腳，她一步也沒有停下。跟在她身後的我，心中讚歎這位嫁入豪門的大媳婦，竟是如此腳踏實地、按部就班、堅持到底的傳遞著洪家企業家的風範！那天之後所有的團員都叫她簡阿姨！直到現在，簡阿姨頂著一頭白髮仍然給予優人智慧的指引，在關鍵時刻幫助我們度過難關！感恩陪伴我們成長的簡阿姨！

蔣顯斌

CNEX 視納華仁聯合創辦人暨董事長

我是在 1975 年，洪建全基金會成立視聽圖書館的那一年，走進這個天地的。

當年如果你也曾踏足此處，也許會看到許多小朋友興奮地看書、聽故事，卻又因為身在圖書館不得不輕聲說著悄悄話。在一個個錄音機前聽故事聽到出神的孩子中，其中有一個，就是當時年僅六、七歲的我。記憶中，我不僅是對每個故事聽得出神，而且對自己能在這小天地獨當一面，決定挑選租借錄音帶、錄影帶與耳機，完成一個小大人探索世界的初體驗，太美妙。因為是啟蒙，至今已經四十五年了，心中的溫度仍格外清晰。數十年後，我斜槓於科技創業與紀錄片文化之路，與簡老師及洪裕鈞更加熟悉。五年前有幸受敏隆講堂之邀，分享紀錄片領域的體驗與思考，經常回想起童年遇上的那顆種籽，可謂殊勝因緣。我感覺到這一顆顆善念的種籽，因著土地與時間的滋養，默默在茫茫人海中抽芽，生養不息。感恩播種之手，處世界之熙來攘往，從不負初衷。

簡文彬

衛武營國家藝術文化中心藝術總監

交響樂團的聲音多而豐富，想要成為一位稱職的指揮，必須有能力「聆聽」。1983 到 1988 年，就讀國立藝專的時期，洪建全視聽圖書館是我「聆聽」的重要資料庫。雖然我多次在偉大的錄音陪伴下酣酣入眠，但那些在無意識間流入我腦海裡的聲音，彷彿一直陪伴著我。直到現在，每每經過中華路、愛國西路口時，我總會下意識地抬起頭，想再看一眼那些已不復存在的樓與人。謝謝基金會的理念，謝謝林宜勝館長，謝謝簡哥及好多人。

Liu Ruoyu

Founder, U-Theatre and U-Theatre Art & Culture Foundation
Chairman of the Taipei Performing Arts Center

The Hongs have always had a knack for discovering
new and ingenious ways to translate our everyday
environment into a vehicle for social development
and growth! After university graduation, the Hong
Foundation's sponsorship of Lanling Theatre Workshop's
Springtime Ballads Concert was the first time I had ever
heard of a private foundation sponsoring performance
art. Years later, after founding U-Theatre, our troupe was
invited to perform at the Paris Quartier d'Ete and go on
a 'yunjiao' (*cloud feet*, meaning walking barefoot) ramble
across France. I invited Celia Hong Chien Chinghui to
come with us. I honestly expected that Celia would use
her time to vacation in Paris rather than join our yunjiao.
I never imagined that she would do the entire, five-day
yunjiao journey with us, barefoot across the undulating
French landscape. Following her those five days gave me
a deep and abiding respect for this women who married
into the Hong family. Her pragmatism, dedication, and
persistence truly convey the best qualities of the Hong
family business. From that day forward all in our troupe
have respectfully called her Auntie Chien. To this day,
Auntie Chien, albeit now with a head of silver-white
hair, continues to give U-Theatre her wise and insightful
guidance and still provides assistance whenever we need
a helping hand! I express my deep gratitude to she who
has grown with us - Auntie Chien!

Ben Tsiang

Co-Founder and Chairman of CNEX

My introduction to the Hong Foundation was in 1975 - the
year they opened their audiovisual library. Had you been
there with me, you too would have seen the gaggle of
kids excitedly reading books and listening to stories and,
because it was a library after all, excitedly conversing in
whispered tones. One of those kids sitting in a cubicle
and listening in rapt attention to stories on audiotape was
me ... about 7 years old at the time. As I remember it, it
wasn't just the stories that amazed me. It was also the
fact that I was allowed to choose for myself which tapes
and videos to borrow. This was a milestone in younger
me's life. It was incredible! Because this was such a
seminal experience, the memories still remain brilliantly
crisp and warm in my mind some forty-five years on.
Several decades later, I launched into a "slash career"
(multi-faceted career) that saw me both involved in a tech
startup and producing cultural documentaries. This work
made me even more familiar with Celia and Royce Hong.
Five years ago, it was my honor to be invited to share
my documentary-filmmaking experience and insights at
Minlong Forum. I regularly think back on the seeds that
the Hong Foundation sowed in my life so many years ago.
For me, it was a gift of karmic proportions. These good
seeds, nourished by good soil and time, have sprouted
and grown robustly. Thank you to the sowers of these
seeds for holding so true to their founding mission!

Chien Wenpin

General and Artistic Director of the National Kaohsiung
Center for the Arts (Weiwuying)

Symphonic orchestral music is resonant and rich. Those
wanting to pursue a career as a music conductor must
first become adept at 'listening'. From 1983 to 1988,
while a student at National Taiwan Academy of Arts,
I found the Hong Foundation's Audiovisual Library an
indispensable resource in training up my own 'listening'
acumen. Although I must admit to nodding off more
than a few times with the majestic sounds of those
audiotapes lilting in my ear, it is those selfsame sounds
that wove their way indelibly into my mental fabric and
that have accompanied me ever since. To this very day,
whenever I pass the corner of Chunghwa and Aiguo East
Roads, I can't help but look up in hopes of glimpsing once
more the long-demolished former offices of the Hong
Foundation and its staff. Thank you for the foundation's
inspired ideas. Thank you to Head Librarian Katz Lynn.
Thank you to my good friend Chien and to so many
others.

洪觀時代
TRANSFORMING VISIONS

前言

「台灣家電拓荒者」洪建全先生打造的「國際牌」，是家喻戶曉、陪伴台灣經濟社會同步成長的關鍵企業，更是生活在台灣的我們，所擁有的共同記憶。

1971年，洪建全基金會成立，簡靜惠執行長將文化帶入洪家事業版圖，於是台灣第一本專業書評雜誌《書評書目》、第一個兒童文學創作獎、第一個視聽圖書館接連成立；第一張現代民歌唱片出版、雲門舞集舞作《白蛇傳》的原創音樂錄製皆獲支持贊助；創立如民間書院的

敏隆講堂、以台灣 PHP 素直友會讀書會推動閱讀⋯⋯在在都是以文化深植在台灣社會進展的歷史裡。

如今，第三代洪裕鈞與張淑征，傳承文化基因，將以創新精神的 HAX 計畫帶領洪建全金會走向下一個五十年⋯⋯

洪建全基金會的五十年，也是台灣的五十年，透過經典而珍貴的照片影像，我們一起觀看過去，觀看現在，觀向時代⋯⋯

贊助雲門舞集舞作《白蛇傳》原創音樂

Sponsored production of original music for Cloud Gate
Dance Theatre's *The Tale of the White Serpent*

創辦洪建全基金會

The Hong Foundation
established

出版楊弦《中國現代民歌集》唱片

Yang Hsien's first album *Contemporary
Taiwanese Folk Music* released

成立文經學苑

The Culture For Business
Academy established

1971 — **1972** — **1974** — **1975** — **1984** — **1987**

出版《書評書目》

*Shu Ping Shu Mu
Review of Books
and Bibliography*
published

成立視聽圖書館

The Hong Foundation
Audiovisual Library opened

成立台灣 PHP 素直友會

Taiwan PHP Sunao
Community founded

設立洪建全兒童文學創作獎

The Hong Foundation Award for
Children's Literature established

Panasonic Taiwan, the renowned company started by "Taiwan's home appliance pioneer" Hong Chienchuan (C.C.), is integral to Taiwan's economic and social development. His "Guojipai" (國際牌) brand still exists as a shared memory among us living in Taiwan.

With the establishment of the Hong Foundation in 1971, Executive Director Celia Hong Chien Chinghui began the process of interweaving culture with the Hong family business. The foundation's subsequent endeavors were all deeply rooted in the cultural fabric of Taiwanese society: it launched Taiwan's first professional book review magazine *Shu Ping Shu Mu*; established Taiwan's first award for children's literature; opened Taiwan's first audiovisual library; sponsored the release of the first contemporary folk music album and the production of original music for

Cloud Gate Dance Theatre *The Tale of the White Serpent*; founded the Minlong Forum, a public learning space; and promoted reading through Taiwan PHP Sunao Community book club meetings.

Now, third-generation leaders Royce YC Hong and Grace Cheung are poised to lead the Hong Foundation into the next half-century with their coming HAX initiative, to continue the foundation's mission of transmitting the genetic codes of culture.

The 50-year history of the Hong Foundation is also a reflection of the past 50 years in Taiwan. Through the following compilation of images, let us reminisce together upon our past, gaze upon our present, and look towards our future.

HAX 啟動下一個 50 年發展引擎

HAX initiative launched to set the Hong Foundation in motion for the next fifty ye.

洪建全與
國際牌傳奇

HONG CHIENCHUAN
AND HIS LEGACY

1964 年，國際牌結合 National 的龐大立方型紅色霓虹燈塔，開始豎立在西門町中華商場屋頂，成為台北城的地標，也是台灣人對於現代文明的想望，都會生活的共同記憶，更見證了洪家事業的奮然崛起。

李悌欽攝影 (1960-1970) / 國立臺灣美術館 國家攝影文化中心典藏

In 1964, the neon signage display bearing the "Guojipai" (國際牌) and "National" brand that stood tall on the rooftop of the Chunghwa Market in Ximending was a landmark for the city of Taipei. It was an emblem for Taiwanese people of an aspiring modern society, a collective memory for citizens of Taipei, and a testament to the rise of the Hong family business.

Photographer: Li Tichin (1960-1970); collection of National Center of Photography and Images, National Taiwan Museum of Fine Arts

洪建全（1913-1986）從白手起家的礦工之子到被譽為「台灣家電業拓荒者」，是冒險犯難、不畏艱辛、認真堅毅的創業家。

1946 年，台灣光復後第二年，洪建全在衡陽路置產，創立「建隆行」，取其名字中的「建」與長子洪敏隆的「隆」。從經營個人商店轉成貿易商行，行銷各種電器產品與貿易批發業務。1949 年，建隆行開始與日本松下電器往來，從日本進口電器到台灣銷售。日本松下在二戰後，接到的第一筆訂單就是建隆行開出的，這成為洪家國際關係企業的啟航，也是奠定兩家公司合作的情誼與基礎。

A coal miner's son who build his business from scratch, Hong Chienchuan (C.C.) (1913-1986) went on to become an enterprising and fearless entrepreneur, renowned as the pioneer for the home appliances industry in Taiwan.

In 1946, the second year of Taiwan's retrocession from colonial rule by Japan, Hong founded Chien Long Company on Hengyang Road, naming it after himself and his eldest son Minlong (M.L.). The shop later became a trading goods store, retailing and distributing all kinds of electronic products. Three years later, Chien Long began doing business with Matsushita Electric Industrial Company (now Panasonic Corporation), importing Japanese electronics to Taiwan. For Matsushita, the purchase order from Chien Long was its first after World War II; whereas for Chien Long, this was the starting point and the foundation for international collaboration between the two companies.

下：建隆行的曲線屋頂造型
右頁
上：洪建全在辦公室
左下：設址在台北市衡陽路 43 號的建隆行，左為洪建全。台灣松下電器提供
右下：洪建全與妻子洪游勉懷抱著長子洪敏隆和次子洪敏弘。

Below: The distinctive roof line of Chien Long Company
Right page
Top: Hong Chienchuan at the office
Bottom left: Chien Long Company at No. 43 Hengyang Road in Taipei City, Hong Chienchuan on the left (photo credit: Panasonic Taiwan)
Bottom right: Hong Chienchuan with his wife Hong Yumein cradling their eldest son Minlong (left) and second son Minhoung (right) in 1941

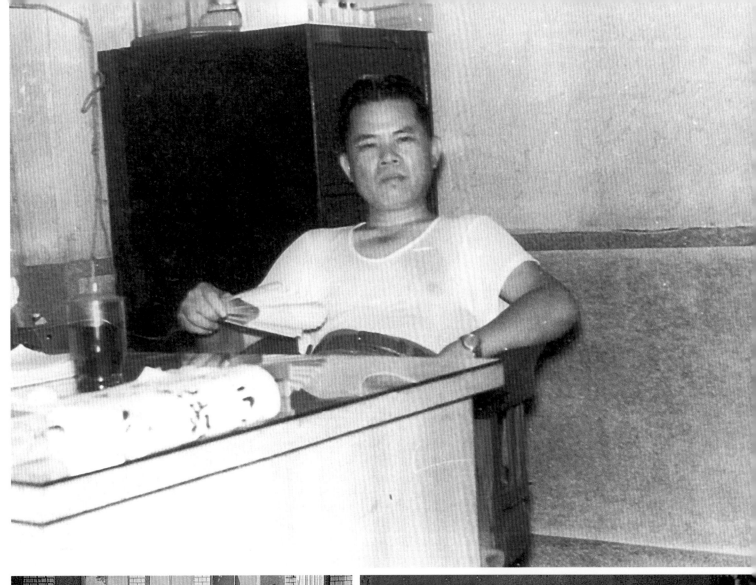

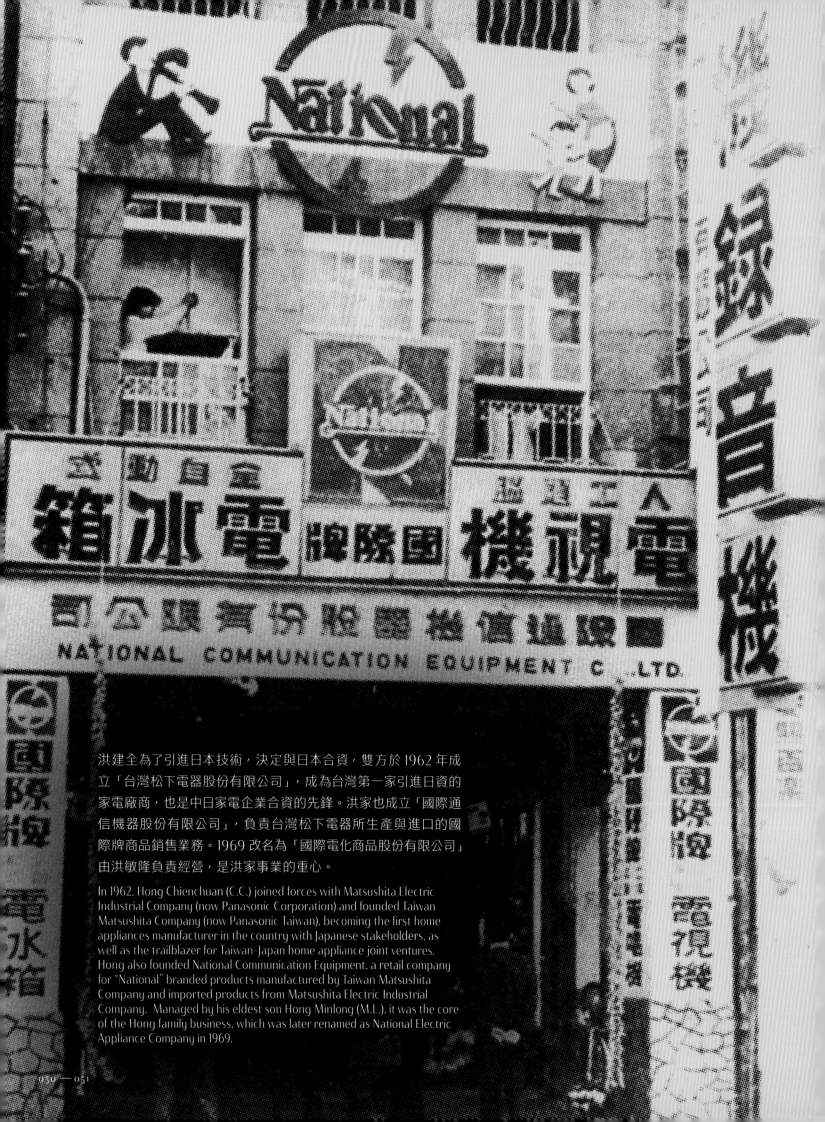

洪建全為了引進日本技術，決定與日本合資，雙方於 1962 年成立「台灣松下電器股份有限公司」，成為台灣第一家引進日資的家電廠商，也是中日家電企業合資的先鋒。洪家也成立「國際通信機器股份有限公司」，負責台灣松下電器所生產與進口的國際牌商品銷售業務。1969 改名為「國際電化商品股份有限公司」由洪敏隆負責經營，是洪家事業的重心。

In 1962, Hong Chienchuan (C.C.) joined forces with Matsushita Electric Industrial Company (now Panasonic Corporation) and founded Taiwan Matsushita Company (now Panasonic Taiwan), becoming the first home appliances manufacturer in the country with Japanese stakeholders, as well as the trailblazer for Taiwan-Japan home appliance joint ventures. Hong also founded National Communication Equipment, a retail company for "National" branded products manufactured by Taiwan Matsushita Company and imported products from Matsushita Electric Industrial Company. Managed by his eldest son Hong Minlong (M.L.), it was the core of the Hong family business, which was later renamed as National Electric Appliance Company in 1969.

1953 年，國民政府為發展台灣經濟，推出第一次「四年經建計劃」，同年，洪建全買下博愛路 57 號的產業，將建隆行改為「建隆電器廠」，開始裝配收音機、製造零件，取代進口產品。洪家從經營商行改以建造工廠生產家電，所生產的第一部收音機，就以「國際牌」為商標名稱，顯見洪建全已有從台灣邁向國際的雄心。

1956 年，洪建全為精益求精、提升產品品質，數次赴日洽商，與日本松下電器產業株式會社社長松下幸之助簽訂技術合作協定，由日方派技術顧問來台指導，也安排台灣技術人員赴日學習，這項合作是台灣產業界的創舉。

In 1953, the same year that the central government introduced the Four-Year Plan for Economic Development, Hong bought the property on No. 57 Boai Road and changed Chien Long Company to Chien Long Manufacturing, assembling radios and manufacturing machine parts in place of imported goods. The family business shifted gear from commercial trade to building factories and manufacturing its own home appliance products. The first radio made used "Guojipai" (國際牌) as its trademark, displaying Hong's ambition to make way onto the international stage.

In 1956, Hong Chienchuan traveled frequently to Japan in search of solutions to improve product quality. He signed a technical collaboration agreement with Konosuke Matsushita, president of Matsushita Electric Industrial Company (now Panasonic Corporation), in which the Japanese partner would send technical advisors to Taiwan and provide training sessions, while Taiwan could send technicians to Japan for training. The collaboration was a truly groundbreaking achievement for Taiwan then.

台灣國際牌創辦人洪建全與日本經營之神也是日本松下電器創辦人松下幸之助，是在漫天烽火過後，攜手走過慘澹歲月，患難見真情，一起打造出台日兩地電器企業的大創業家。台灣松下電器提供
Hong Chienchuan and Konosuke Matsushita, founder of Matsushita Electric Industrial (now Panasonic Corporation) – two entrepreneurs who reached out to one another in times of turmoil and desolation after the war to build an electronics empire across two countries. (photo credit: Panasonic Taiwan)

1956 年 5 月，洪建全創辦人（左二）與松下幸之助先生
簽訂技術合作協定的簽約儀式。台灣松下電器提供
May 1956 signing ceremony between Hong Chienchuan (second from left)
and Matsushita Electric Industrial (now Panasonic Corporation) founder
Konosuke Matsushita marking the start of their formal collaboration.
(photo credit: Panasonic Taiwan)

1962 年設廠於新北市中和區的台灣松下電器公司。
圖為總部全景 台灣松下電器提供
1962 bird's eye view of the headquarters and
manufacturing plant (now Panasonic Taiwan) in Zhonghe
District, New Taipei City (photo credit: Panasonic Taiwan)

左：台灣松下電器徽章，使用至 2008 年
中：國際牌徽章，自創業使用至 1971 年
右：國際牌＋台灣松下電器徽章，1971 年後使用至 2003 年
圖片皆為台灣松下電器提供

Left: Taiwan Matsushita insignia, used until 2008
Middle: "Guojipai" and National brand insignia (1962 - 1971)
Right: National brand and Taiwan Matsushita insignia (1971 - 2003)
(photo credits: Panasonic Taiwan)

1956 年，洪建全為因應市場需求擴建廠房，將建隆電器廠遷移至中和，改名為「國際通信機械股份有限公司」。在尚未與日方合資前，生意就非常興盛；合資後，繼續以「國際牌」為品牌，更如虎添翼，也加速進階到現代化生活。

洪建全鼓勵自製與創新，1962 年，台灣松下電器的「第一台」產品陸續問世，第一台真空管收音機 GU-263，讓國際牌聲名大噪，接著推出第一台電唱機 (1962)、第一台電鍋 (1963 年 9 月)、第一台電視機 (1963 年 11 月)、第一台烤麵包機 (1965 年 5 月)、第一台電冰箱 (1965 年 6 月)、第一台洗衣機 (1967 年 4 月) …… 台灣每個家庭都希望有國際牌家電產品，自此在坊間有「大家的國際牌」之稱。圖片皆為台灣松下電器提供

In 1956, Hong Chienchuan moved Chien Long Manufacturing to Zhonghe to increase production capacity and meet market demand, changing its name to National Communication Equipment. Already making booming business, Hong took business to the next level after the joint venture with Japan, and pioneered the industrial development in Taiwan.

Hong championed in-house manufacturing and innovation, bringing out firsts of many Panasonic Taiwan products in 1962, including the first vacuum tube radio (which gave the brand its claim to fame), followed by the first record player (1962), the first rice cooker (September 1963), the first television set (November 1963), the first toaster (May 1965), the first refrigerator (June 1965), and the first washing machine (April 1967). At this time, "Guojipai" (國際牌) and "National" brand home appliances were greatly desired or must-have items in every Taiwanese household, hence the highly recognized lingo of "Everyone's Guojipai." (photo credits: Panasonic Taiwan)

只有小學畢業的洪建全，十四歲就出外打天下，從學徒、店長、商行經營者，一路成為台灣松下電器董事長，是促進台灣家電業現代化，也是推動台灣經濟發展的重要推手。曾於 1967 年當選第二屆中華民國十大企業家，也曾榮獲「全國優良商人」(1978) 和當選「模範父親」(1983)。

本著「取之於社會，用之於社會」的精神，於 1971 年成立「洪建全教育文化基金會」，在仍是戒嚴時期的 70 年代，以經濟、以創意、以文化、以教育關懷社會更帶動台灣社會前行。謝春德攝影

Having only been educated in primary school, Hong Chienchuan was already working by the age of fourteen, progressing from apprentice, store manager, owner and all the way to founder and chairman of Taiwan Matsushita. Not only did Hong facilitated the modernization of electronic home appliances in Taiwan, he also played a key part in the development of the country's economy. He was awarded Top Ten Taiwan Entrepreneurs in 1967, National Outstanding Business Leader in 1978, and Model Father in 1983.

In 1971, the Hong Foundation was established bearing the motto "Of the society, for the society," advocating economic progress, creativity, culture and education to lead Taiwan society forward amidst times of martial law. (photographer: Hsieh Chunte)

上：矗立於中華商場的國際牌燈塔，是最鮮明的廣告標示，圖為各界慶祝第四任總統、副總統就職大典時的公告即在人口往來密集的國際牌燈塔之下。中央社 1966 年，中央通訊社提供
下：祖孫三代：洪建全、洪敏隆、洪裕鈞都分別在 1964、1987、2016 年擔任台灣松下電器董事長。

Top: The "Guojipai" and "National" brand billboard tower atop the bustling Chunghwa Market was an urban landmark. Here, the billboard showed a celebration message on the inauguration of Taiwan's fourth President and Vice President. (photo published by the Central News Agency in 1966; photo credit: CNA)
Bottom: Three generations of the Hongs: Hong Chienchuan (C.C.), Hong Minlong (M.L.), and Royce YC Hong have each served and still serves as Chairman of Panasonic Taiwan from 1964-1987, 1987-1990, and 2016-present respectively.

洪建全曾獲時任行政院院長蔣經國頒發「富國裕民」獎牌（1977年6月），這時的台灣開始從農業社會轉向工業社會，人民生活水平尚待提升，企業經營正要萌芽。洪建全與日本松下合作，希望讓民眾享用最先進的電器用品。為確保服務品質，積極引進日方制度如企業管理、經銷商制度、衛星工廠育成及員工福利措施等，如員工運動大會、週休二日等制度……創下當時台灣企業風氣之先，也早在政府推動時就已先施行。洪建全被稱為「帶出日式管理特色的台灣企業家」，為台灣企業發展建立優質典範。

事業興盛的洪建全時時想要回饋社會，更認為人才教育的培養要從學校開始。

1979年10月，捐贈五百萬元給台灣大學設立電子電路研究室，洪建全與台大校長閻振興進行簽約儀式（左）。為協助發展電子通信科學教育，捐贈儀器給台大「電磁波實驗室」（右）。

In June 1977, Hong Chienchuan received a medal of Honor from Taiwan's former President Chiang Chingkuo, who was then Head of the Executive Yuan, in praise of his contribution in enriching and prospering the country and its people. It was a time when Taiwan was about to transition from an agricultural society to an industrial society– when living standards were in need of improvement, and businesses were seeing rapid growth. Hong's collaboration with Panasonic Japan aspired to bring state-of-the-art home appliances to Taiwan consumers. To ensure the quality of service, he introduced Japanese systems such as business management know how, retail strategy, incubation of satellite factories, employee benefits such as company sports day and five-day working week, etc., which had never been seen in Taiwanese companies, and thus was way ahead of the central government in their policy implementation. Hong Chienchuan became known as "a Taiwanese entrepreneur who managed his business the Japanese way," and served as a role model for Taiwan's business development.

As Hong Chienchuan continued to strive in business, he wanted to give back to the society, as he believed that the nurturing of talents begins in school. Hong joined National Taiwan University (NTU) President Yen Chenhsing at the signing ceremony marking the donation of NT$5 million to establish the NTU Electronic Circuits Lab (left) in October 1979. Donated equipment at the NTU Electronic Circuits Lab for the advancement of the electronic & communication sciences (right).

上：1975 年 10 月，洪建全（右）陪同嚴家淦總統（中）
參觀電子展覽，巡視國際牌攤位。
下：1971 年 3 月，行政院副院長蔣經國（前排中）
蒞臨台灣松下電器視察，洪建全陪同在旁（前排右）。
圖片皆為台灣松下電器提供

Top: Hong Chienchuan (right) accompanies Taiwan President Yen Chiakan (middle)
on his visit to the Panasonic Taiwan booth at the Electronics Fair in October 1975.
Bottom: Vice Premier of the Executive Yuan (and future Taiwan President) Chiang
Chingkuo (center front) on an inspection tour of Panasonic Taiwan accompanied
by Hong Chienchuan (center right). (photo credits: Panasonic Taiwan)

台灣松下電器的生產線上不停運轉著，持續產出收音機、電唱機、揚聲器、電晶體收音機、電鍋、黑白電視機、四聲道立體收音機、電唱機、彩色電視機、洗衣機等，成為當時家電業的領導品牌。

台灣松下電器更是台灣第一家電視機製造商，1963 年推出的第一台 16 吋真空管黑白電視機，剛好因應台灣第一家電視台──台視的開播而上市；1969 年推出的「金龍電視機」以響亮的命名回應金龍少棒隊揚名海外，更是陪伴國人徹夜不眠、一同看少棒轉播的共同記憶與黃金年代……

As assembly lines continued to roll out new models of radios, record players, stereos, transistor radios, rice cookers, black-and-white and color television sets, quadraphonic radios, washing machines, etc., Panasonic Taiwan had become the leading brand in home appliances.

The manufacturer of Taiwan's first television sets, Panasonic Taiwan also introduced the first 16-inch vacuum tube black-and-white television set in 1963, the same time that the country's first television channel TTV went on air. The Golden Dragon Television introduced in 1969 was a tribute to the Taiwan baseball team of the same name; those who grew up in the 60's and 70's share the memory of that one summer night when everyone stayed up late to watch the Golden Dragon baseball team win the Little League World Baseball Championships on television.

左：國際牌電視機的生產線
右上：國際牌黑膠播放機
右下：國際牌電器展示中心，
有最先進的各項電器產品。
圖片皆為台灣松下電器提供

Left: Taiwan Matsushita production lines
(photo credit: Panasonic Taiwan)
Top right: "National" brand vinyl record players
Bottom: The company's electronics
showroom displaying the latest products
(photo credits: Panasonic Taiwan)

上：1977 年，因創辦《書評書目》雜誌等文化事業，榮獲第七屆「十大傑出女青年獎」，頒獎當天全家都來祝賀。
下：忙碌工作中的簡靜惠　光華雜誌提供
Top: Celia Hong Chien Chinghui was awarded the 7th Top Ten Outstanding Women of Taiwan in 1977 for her work in *Shu Ping Shu Mu Review of Books and Bibliography* and other cultural sponsorships.
Bottom: Celia at work (photo credit: Taiwan Panorama magazine)

1971 年，台灣退出聯合國，當時全國陷入不安，但洪建全卻在此刻以更大的胸懷，以文化與教育扎根台灣，成立「洪建全教育文化基金會」，由長媳簡靜惠擔任首任執行長。簡靜惠是台大歷史系畢業，美國羅耀拉大學教育研究所碩士；有著歷史與教育的學歷背景，同時擔任家族企業的財務經理與基金會執行長；她熱愛閱讀與人文，將文化理念帶入洪家事業版圖，以「上午營利，下午非營利」的工作模式，一腳在企業一腳在文化。直至 1990 年，丈夫洪敏隆過世後，將全部心力投入洪建全基金會。她長期關懷台灣藝術文化的發展並持續深耕，以素直心推廣閱讀並經營讀書會群。由簡靜惠帶領的洪建全基金會五十年，在台灣文化界創下許多的「第一」……

In 1971, as the whole country was rattled by the government's withdrawal from the United Nations, Hong Chienchuan established the Hong Foundation, with the aim of supporting the country through culture and education. Celia Hong Chien Chinghui was appointed the foundation's first Executive Director. Juggling this position with the role of finance manager in the family business, Chien acquired a "profit in the morning, non-profit in the afternoon" working style, bringing in cultural advocacies drawn from her academic background in history and education. Many "firsts" innovations were seen in the 50 years that Hong led the foundation.

謝春德攝影
(photographer: Hsieh Chunte)

台灣第一本專業書評雜誌《書評書目》1972-1981
THE FIRST BOOK REVIEW MAGAZINE IN TAIWAN –
SHU PING SHU MU

吉鳳行

順賀國際有限公司

SHANNON INTERNATIONAL CORP.

1972 年 9 月，台灣第一本專業書評雜誌《書評書目》誕生了，當時的辦公室在博愛路國際電化公司的三樓小房間。1975 年 9 月，視聽圖書館開幕，書評書目出版社跟著遷移至南京東路三段 96、98 號的二樓。

Shu Ping Shu Mu Review of Books and Bibliography, Taiwan's first book review magazine, was published in September 1972 in a small office on the 3rd floor of the National Electric Appliance Company on Boai Road. In September 1975, The Hong Foundation Audiovisual Library opened its doors at No. 96-98 Nanjing East Road Section 3, where Shu Ping Shu Mu Publishing also relocated to.

書評書目

書評書目
雙月刊
中華民國六十一年九月一日

CRITICISM
CATALOGUE

1972 年 9 月，洪建全基金會出版《書評書目》雜誌，是台灣出版界的創舉，在簡靜惠的奔走，洪敏隆說服洪家鼎力支持，再加上愛書成癖的主編隱地，完成了《書評書目》的構想與正式發行。

這本雜誌源於對知識的崇敬，對出版的熱愛，也是知識份子對社會的責任。首任主編隱地（柯青華）曾說：「《書評書目》雜誌是我生命中的一艘帆船，它曾經航行於書海，為台灣的書評、書介、書目盡力，並報導學人和作家生活，為他們描述，甚至透過小說、散文、寫藏書的故事，讀書的故事，這樣一本以『書』為主角的雜誌，要我一輩子為它獻身，我也是願意的。」

In September 1972, the Hong Foundation published *Shu Ping Shu Mu Review of Books and Bibliography*, the first-ever literary criticism magazine in Taiwan's publishing industry. It was the unceasing hard work of Celia Hong Chien Chinghui along with the editor-in-chief Yin Ti's passion for books, that helped Hong Minlong to persuade the Hong family to support its birth.

This magazine sprang from the creators' respect for knowledge and enthusiasm for publishing, and a social responsibility for intellectuals. Editor-in-chief Ko Chinghwa, aka Yin Ti, said: "*Shu Ping Shu Mu* is a boat of my life crossing the ocean of books, setting sail our contributions of book reviews, book introductions and catalogues; and stories of thinkers, authors, stories of reading and book collections through essays and novels. A publication that focuses on books and books only – I am more than willing to give my entire life to."

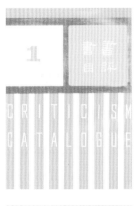

書評書目　BOOK REVIEW AND BIBLIOGRAPHY

・故總統　蔣公書目彙編
・照亮中國古史的人
・民國以來的文學運動集
・評萬全書
・大型刊物亮起了紅燈

25　中華民國六十四年五月一日出版

書評書目 21　中華民國六十年一月一日出版　BOOK REVIEW AND BIBLIOGRAPHY

學術界的奇人・發現一個小說家

書評書目 22　中華民國六十四年二月一日出版　BOOK REVIEW AND BIBLIOGRAPHY

春耕秋收・訪梁實秋教授

書評書目 23　中華民國六十四年三月一日出版　BOOK REVIEW AND BIBLIOGRAPHY

蝴蝶的幼蟲・喜悲的悲憫

書評書目 24　中華民國六十四年四月一日出版　BOOK REVIEW AND BIBLIOGRAPHY

訪吳大猷博士・借書版權費

書評書目 26　中華民國六十四年六月一日出版　BOOK REVIEW AND BIBLIOGRAPHY

徐訏二三事・詩的人特權？

書評書目 27　中華民國六十四年七月一日出版　BOOK REVIEW AND BIBLIOGRAPHY

山河歲月話漁樵・余光中：

書評書目 28　中華民國六十四年八月一日出版　BOOK REVIEW AND BIBLIOGRAPHY

書評書目 29　中華民國六十四年九月一日出版　BOOK REVIEW AND BIBLIOGRAPHY

創刊三周年紀念・諾貝爾文學獎秘史

書評書目 30　中華民國六十四年十月一日出版　BOOK REVIEW AND BIBLIOGRAPHY

書評書目 31　中華民國六十四年十一月一日出版　BOOK REVIEW AND BIBLIOGRAPHY

書評書目 32　中華民國六十四年十二月一日出版　BOOK REVIEW AND BIBLIOGRAPHY

書評書目 33　中華民國65年1月1日出版　BOOK REVIEW AND BIBLIOGRAPHY

家庭書目：讓我們一起來讀書

書評書目 34　中華民國65年2月1日出版　BOOK REVIEW AND BIBLIOGRAPHY

書評書目 35　中華民國65年3月1日出版　BOOK REVIEW AND BIBLIOGRAPHY

談英國散文選・英語重逢記

書評書目 36　中華民國65年4月1日出版　BOOK REVIEW AND BIBLIOGRAPHY

書評書目 37　中華民國65年5月1日出版　BOOK REVIEW AND BIBLIOGRAPHY

書評書目 38　中華民國65年6月1日出版　BOOK REVIEW AND BIBLIOGRAPHY

書評書目 39　中華民國65年7月1日出版　BOOK REVIEW AND BIBLIOGRAPHY

從台北人的缺失談起・新女性和她們的書

書評書目 40　中華民國65年8月1日出版　BOOK REVIEW AND BIBLIOGRAPHY

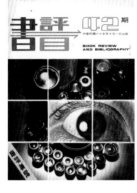

BOOK REVIEW AND BIBLIOGRAPHY
中華民國66年2月1日出版

書評書目

46

1977 年 2 月號（第 46 期）的《書評書目》，刊出一篇來自香港評論家清淮所寫〈於梨華的新書〉一文，發行上架沒多久，便接到警備總部的「關切」。

在那個戒嚴時代，出版言論受控制，主編只好帶著同仁，跑到重慶南路、武昌街、博愛路等書店和書報攤，向店家說明原委，拿起雜誌，撕去此文，再放回書架上。

當年發行《書評書目》這樣純粹的雜誌，卻得承受政治壓力，讓基金會蒙上陰影，對日後停刊不無影響。

When Vol. 46 of *Shu Ping Shu Mu Review of Books and Bibliography* was published in February 1977, the publisher took a "call of concern" from the Taiwan Garrison Command not long after its distribution, as the magazine featured areview by Hong Kong critic Ching Jun on the latest piece of writing by Yu Lihua.

As Taiwan was still under martial law during that time, strict control of publications was exercised, so the editor-in-chief had to send colleagues to rip out the page containing the review in every magazine that was on every shelf in every bookshop and every bookstall on Chongqing South Road, Wuchang Street and Boai Road.

What started merely as a literary publication had to now carry such political pressure, casting a shadow on the Hong Foundation which later ceased the magazine publication.

書評書目 61　徐志摩　胡適寫給羅業的信　中華民國六十七年五月一日出版　BOOK REVIEW AND BIBLIOGRAPHY

書評書目 62　專輯 周策縱「五四運動史」　譯書與中國的現代化　生活雜誌的死亡與復生　墨西哥詩人帕斯的世界　中華民國六十七年六月一日出版　BOOK REVIEW AND BIBLIOGRAPHY

書評書目 63　專輯 周策縱「五四運動史」　導讀：報導文學是什麼　墨西哥詩人帕斯的世界　中華民國六十七年七月一日出版　BOOK REVIEW AND BIBLIOGRAPHY

書評書目 64　專輯 怎樣的視聽　怎樣的精神　戲劇工作者談戲劇的現況與前途　評介棋苓嘯的「老人」　中華民國六十七年八月一日出版　BOOK REVIEW AND BIBLIOGRAPHY

書評書目 65　座談會 小說改編電影的問題　本月座談六週年特輯　訪問金耀基·徐矿雄　日本筑摩書房的倒產　中華民國六十七年九月一日出版　BOOK REVIEW AND BIBLIOGRAPHY

書評書目 66　黃文範的翻譯藝術　中華民國六十七年十月一日出版　BOOK REVIEW AND BIBLIOGRAPHY　洪建全教育文化基金會發行

書評書目 67　1978年諾貝爾文學獎得主 以撒·辛格　寒爵報導　中華民國六十七年十一月一日出版　BOOK REVIEW AND BIBLIOGRAPHY　洪建全教育文化基金會發行

書評書目 68　洪建全教育文化基金會發行

書評書目 69　洪建全教育文化基金會發行

書評書目 70　洪建全教育文化基金會發行

書評書目 71　洪建全教育文化基金會發行

書評書目 72　洪建全教育文化基金會發行　旗升　戲遊字數

書評書目 73　BOOK REVIEW AND BIBLIOGRAPHY　中華民國六十八年五月一日出版　洪建全教育文化基金會發行

書評書目 74　中華民國六十八年六月一日出版　洪建全教育文化基金會發行　BOOK REVIEW AND BIBLIOGRAPHY

目書評書 75　洪建全教育文化基金會發行　中華民國六十八年七月一日出版

書評書目 76　洪建全教育文化基金會發行　中華民國六十八年八月一日出版

書評書目 77　BOOK REVIEW AND BIBLIOGRAPHY　中華民國六十八年九月一日出版　洪建全教育文化基金會發行

書評書目 78　洪建全教育文化基金會發行　BOOK REVIEW AND BIBLIOGRAPHY

書評書目 79　洪建全教育文化基金會發行　BOOK REVIEW AND BIBLIOGRAPHY　中華民國六十八年十一月一日出版

書評書目 80　洪建全教育文化基金會發行　BOOK REVIEW AND BIBLIOGRAPHY　中華民國六十八年十二月一日出版

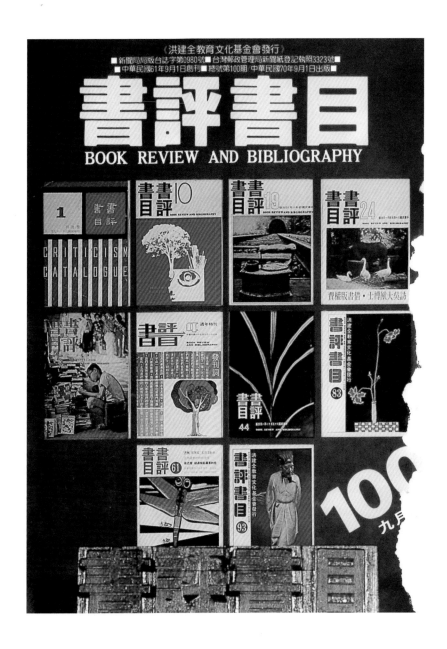

《書評書目》雜誌自 1972 年 9 月第一期出刊至 1981 年 9 月停刊，歷經四位主編：隱地、陳秋坤、王鴻仁、陳恆嘉，經營九年，發行一百期。

在第一百期的〈停刊詞〉中記載：「希望經由雜誌的介紹、批評、關懷及提示，有系統地接受書中新知，使我們的胸襟開闊，眼光看遠，人人都讀書，大家都愛書，使我們的社會是一個『充滿書香』的社會，一片祥和，充滿溫馨，在祥和中深思，《書評書目》雜誌就是在這樣的方針下，一步一步地向前邁進至今。」

Shu Ping Shu Mu Review of Books and Bibliography published Vol. 1 in September 1972, and ended with Vol. 100 in September 1981, managed by four editor-in-chiefs over a period of nine years: Yin Ti, Chen Chiukun, Wang Hongjen, and Chen Hengchia.

In the ending note published in Vol. 100 was written: "We hope that readers had benefited from these literary introductions, pointers, criticisms and analysis; and are willing to take the long view with a more open mind. When everyone reads and loves reading, our society will be filled with the warm, sweet fragrance of books, and we can all ponder our thoughts in peace. That is what has kept *Shu Ping Shu Mu* moving forward to this day."

台灣第一座
視聽圖書館
1975-1989

THE FIRST
AUDIOVISUAL
LIBRARY IN TAIWAN

1975 年，視聽圖書館成立，提供人們一個欣賞音樂的場所，對愛樂人與視聽設備不普及的家庭來說，真是一大福音。在有著豐厚藝術、音樂與人文涵養的林宜勝館長的經營之下，為台灣提高音樂水準與視聽環境；藉著視聽與影像，倡導音樂教育，傳播新經驗。

許多曾在音樂影視發展有成的知名人士都曾是視聽圖書館會員，如導演李安、指揮家簡文彬，與音樂製作人李壽全等人。

In 1975, the Hong Foundation Audiovisual Library was established as a place for people to enjoy music– tremendous good news for music lovers who could not afford to own sound systems. Directed by Katz Lynn, who was well versed in art, music and the humanities, the library aimed to advance the love and appreciation of music through music education and state-of-the-art listening experiences.

Acclaimed director Ang Lee, conductor Chien Wenpin and music producer Lee Shouchuan are some of the many well-known people in the music industry who were once members of the Hong Foundation Audiovisual Library.

左：位於台北市中華路一段 89 之 3 號的洪建全視聽圖書館
右：位於中華路五樓的小型音樂廳
Left: The Hong Foundation Audiovisual Library, located at No. 89-3, Chunghua Road Section 1 in Taipei
Right: The auditorium on the 5th floor of the library

視聽圖書館有著一流的設備,除了一般民眾也是台灣許多作曲家的聚會場所;史惟亮與許常惠在此有小型研究室;許博允、馬水龍、溫隆信、張繼高等知名音樂人,也都常在此地交流。

Furbished with state-of-the-art audiovisual equipment, the library was not only a listening space for the general public, but also a place where Taiwanese composers like Shih Weiliang, Hsu Tsanghouei had their own research labs, and renowned artists such as Hsu Poyun, Ma Shuilong, David Wen Loonghsing and Zhang Jigao could be seen exchanging ideas on music.

左上：視聽圖書館的借閱櫃台
左下：洪建全（左二）與作曲家溫隆信（左一）、馬水龍（右二）、許博允（右一）等人相互交流·
右：視聽圖書館的監視螢幕，顯示著每層樓的使用情況。
Top left: Counter for borrowing materials in the Hong Foundation Audiovisual Library
Bottom left: Hong Chienchuan (second from left) with musicians David Wen Loonghsing (left),
Ma Shuilong (second from right), and Hsu Poyun (right)
Right: Cameras in the Hong Foundation Audiovisual Library facilitated real-time monitoring of each floor

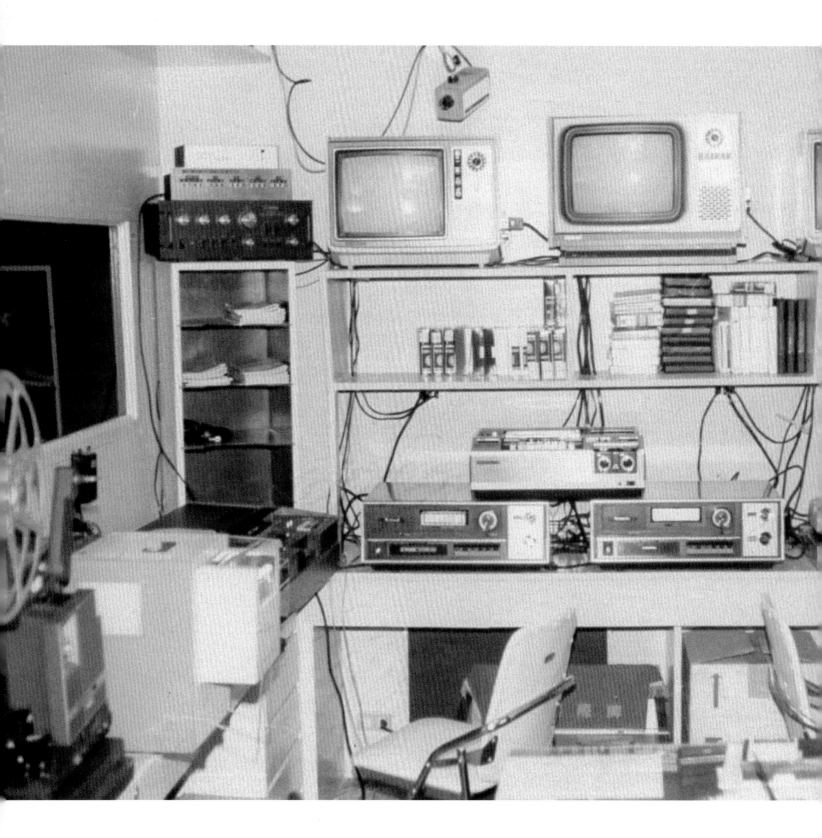

左：視聽圖書館的視聽器材
右：中華路一樓的櫥窗展示新出版的書及國際牌的視聽產品
Left: Equipment at the Hong Foundation Audiovisual Library
Right: Showroom window on Chunghua Road displaying the latest book releases and audiovisual equipment

視聽圖書館中的軟硬體設備多是來自洪家企業的視聽產品，如電視機、錄影機、音響設備等；家族成員如洪敏弘、洪敏昌、洪敏泰喜歡玩音響，也將各自收藏的許多高品質的黑膠唱片捐贈給基金會。

The hardware and software in the library mainly consisted of products manufactured by the Hong family business, such as television sets, video players, sound systems, as well as collector's recordings from the family; Hong's sons Minhoung, Minchung and Mintai who liked to tinker with sound systems donated many high quality vinyl records to the audiovisual collection.

1975 年 9 月,視聽圖書館於台北市南京東路開幕,1977 年 12 月搬至中華路,新館面積是舊館的五倍大。一樓是書評書目辦公室和視聽教育器材展示中心;二樓是兒童閱覽室、兒童文學資料室、兒童視聽室;三樓是閱覽室、研究室、個別錄影觀賞室;四樓是辦公室;五樓是小型音樂廳,設有 120 個座位,可舉辦音樂欣賞、影片欣賞、專題演講等。

視聽圖書館採會員制,國小四年級以上即可申請,學生 100 元,社會人士 150 元,可借閱館內圖書、期刊、錄音帶、錄影帶,還可免費得到《國際視聽月刊》,還可以優惠價格買到基金會出版的書籍唱片及音樂會入場券。

The Hong Foundation Audiovisual Library opened in September 1975 and relocated from Nanjing East Road to Chunghua Road in December 1977, with the new venue five times the size of the old one. The office for Shu Ping Shu Mu Publishing and the audiovisual education equipment display center were on the ground floor; the children's reading room, literature reference room and audiovisual room on the 2nd floor; the reading room, research lab, private video room on the 3rd floor; and the library office on the 4th floor. On the top floor was a 120 seat auditorium suitable for music performances, movie events and lectures.

Membership to the audiovisual library was available to anyone above fourth grade, with a membership fee of NTD$100 for students and NTD$150 for adults. Members were granted access to books, periodicals, audio and video tapes, and would receive the *National Audiovisual Monthly* magazine for free. They could also purchase books and records published by the foundation as well as tickets to concerts organized by the foundation at discounted prices.

左：民眾在閱覽室可自在閱讀
右上：民眾可自行使用視聽設備
右下：位於南京東路上的小型演奏廳
Left: The reading room opened to the general public
Top right: The public using the audiovisual facilities
Bottom right: The auditorium on Nanjing East Road

視聽圖書館是台灣早年重要的音樂教育場域，以音樂文化和兒童教育為主軸，舉辦許多與音樂、藝術、人文相關的課程、小型演奏會，外籍教師授鋼琴等（如左頁圖）。

知名作曲家李泰祥（上）、美學大師蔣勳（下）也曾於此地舉辦講座。

The Hong Foundation Audiovisual Library provided a stage for music education, vital to Taiwanese culture in the early years. The library organized many events related to music, arts and humanities, focusing on advocating music culture and children's education, including mini concerts, international piano tutors, etc. (left page).

Renowned composer Lee Taihsiang (top) and Chiang Hsun (bottom), the authority on aesthetics, also held lectures at the library.

民歌時代
THE AGE OF FOLK MUSIC

洪建全基金會執行長簡靜惠支持如楊弦等民歌手「唱我們自己的歌」，認為這是找尋自我的認同與文化的認同，意義非比尋常。民歌之母陶曉清說：「創作現代民歌是一條剛剛走出來的路，這一顆種籽也才剛剛埋入土中，這裡有一群打先鋒的人，在這起步時期，他們都願意不斷地試驗，不斷地改進，而推動它最有效的途徑就是出版唱片。」於是基金會出資錄製楊弦的《中國現代民歌集》，這是台灣第一張民歌唱片的出版，自此推動了現代民歌風潮。

Celia Hong Chien Chinghui, Executive Director of the Hong Foundation, supported folk singers such as Yang Hsien to "Sing Our Own Songs," believing that it is of extraordinary significance to search for one's own identity and culture. "The creation of contemporary folk music is a road that's only just been walked on, a seed that has only just been planted by undaunted experimental pioneers who are willing to take risks to make lasting changes, and the best way to push this forward is to make records," said Cora Tao, the Mother of Taiwanese Folk Music. The Hong Foundation funded the recording of Yang Hsien's album *Contemporary Taiwanese Folk Music*, the first folk album released in Taiwan, and which kick started the new wave of contemporary folk music.

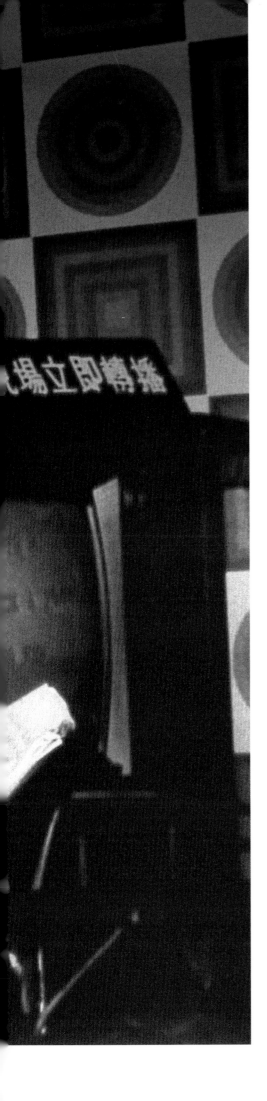

右：許多民歌手也在視聽圖書館舉辦演唱會，如楊弦（上）、
王夢麟和趙樹海（左下）和任祥（右下）。
左：民歌之母陶曉清在視聽圖書館。

Right: Yang Hsien (top), Wang Monling and Allen Chao (bottom left), and Jen Xiang (bottom right) were several of the many folk musicians who performed at the Hong Foundation Audiovisual Library.
Left: Cora Tao, the Mother of Taiwanese Folk Music at the library

簡靜惠曾表示基金會從來沒有出版唱片與發行的經驗，但她憑著一股熱誠認為這是應該做的事，大膽創新與嘗試，且不計盈虧，接連出版了好幾張膾炙人口的音樂唱片。其中《陳達和他的歌》榮獲首屆金鼎獎「唱片類」獎項。

《中國現代民歌集》(1975 年 8 月)
《中國當代音樂作品》(1976 年 9 月)
《西出陽關》(1977 年 4 月)
《陳達和他的歌》(1977 年 5 月)
《我們的歌 1》(1977 年 10 月)
《我們的歌 2》(1977 年 10 月)
《我們的歌 3》(1978 年 7 月)
《中國民間音樂 1》(1978 年 2 月)
《中國民間音樂 2》(1978 年 2 月)
《中國民間音樂 3》(1978 年 2 月)
《童年的回憶》(1981 年)

Celia Hong Chien had no experience in the publication of music records, yet based on a hunch, and believing that it was the right thing to do, she took the challenge and published a number of hit records with no regard to profitability; among these recordings, *Chen Da and His Songs* ended up winning the first Golden Tripod Award (record category).

Contemporary Taiwanese Folk Music (August 1975)
Contemporary Taiwanese Music Works (September 1976)
West Beyond Yang Pass (April 1977)
A Folk Musician: Chen Da and His Songs (October 1977)
Our Songs, Vol. 1 (October 1977)
Our Songs, Vol. 2 (October 1977)
Our Songs, Vol. 3 (July 1978)
Taiwanese Folk Music Collection, Vol. 1 (February 1978)
Taiwanese Folk Music Collection, Vol. 2 (February 1978)
Taiwanese Folk Music Collection, Vol. 3 (February 1978)
Childhood Memories (1981)

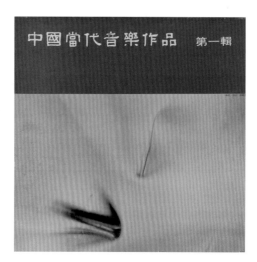

許常惠主編／EDITED BY HSU TSANG-HOUEI

中國民間音樂

第一輯：第一屆民間樂人音樂會選粹

CHINESE FOLK-MUSIC
VOLUME I: HIGH-LIGHT FROM THE 1ST FOLK-MUSIC CONCERT

許常惠主編／EDITED BY HSU TSANG-HOUEI

中國民間音樂

第二輯：第二屆民間樂人音樂會選粹

CHINESE FOLK-MUSIC
VOLUME II: HIGH-LIGHT FROM THE 2ND FOLK-MUSIC CONCERT

許常惠主編／EDITED BY HSU TSANG-HOUEI

中國民間音樂

第三輯：第三屆民間樂人音樂會選粹

CHINESE FOLK-MUSIC
VOLUME III: HIGH-LIGHT FROM THE 3RD FOLK-MUSIC CONCERT

策劃　陶曉清

我們的歌

中國創作民歌系列

3

台灣鄉土
老調．新聲
童年的回憶
簡上仁　作品專集
李泰祥　編曲．指揮
台灣童謠：遊戲．搖籃．
幻想．連珠組曲

支持
民俗音樂採集
THE COLLECTION OF
INDIGENOUS MUSIC

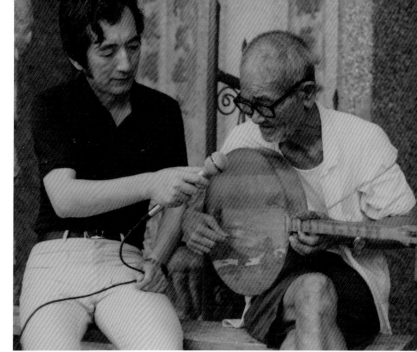

1975 年開始，基金會資助許常惠調查與出版台灣傳統音樂研究。史惟亮先生英年早逝之後，基金會繼續支持許常惠的民俗音樂採集計畫，並在新成立的視聽圖書館提供資料室、定期舉辦音樂講座、音樂會等。陸續發掘出多位民間藝人，譬如民歌手陳達、歌仔戲第一苦旦廖瓊枝、布袋戲藝師李天祿等人。

Since 1975, the Hong Foundation has funded musician Hsu Tsanghouei in his research and publication of Taiwanese indigenous music. After the early death of composer Shih Weiliang, the foundation continued to support Hsu, providing him access to the audiovisual library's data trove, and organizing regular lectures and concerts. In turn, the foundation also discovered music giants such as folk singer Chen Da, Taiwanese opera lead "Kudan" (female role for melodrama) Liao Chiungchih and Taiwanese puppet master Lee Tienlu.

左：史惟亮（左）與許常惠（右）
許常惠文化藝術基金會提供
下：亞洲作曲家聯盟第四屆大會頒給洪建全基金會的贊助感謝狀（1976 年）
Left: Shih Weiliang (left) and Hsu Tsanghouei (right)
(photo credit: Tsang-Houei Hsu Cultural and Art Foundation)
Bottom: Certificate of Appreciation presented to the Hong Foundation at the 4th Asian Composers League (ACL) Conference

上：許常惠發掘了許多民間藝人，陳達是其中之一。
中：許常惠採集泰雅族音樂。
下：至花蓮縣卓溪鄉卓溪村採集布農族音樂（1978 年）。
圖片皆為許常惠文化藝術基金會提供

Top: Hsu Tsanghouei helped bring many folk artists, including Chen Da, to nationwide audiences.
Middle: Hsu Tsanghouei recording aboriginal Atayal music
Bottom: Hsu Tsanghouei recording a live performance of aboriginal Bunun songs in Zhuoxi, Hualien County (1978)
(photo credits: Tsang-Houei Hsu Cultural and Art Foundation)

陳達
和他的歌
CHEN DA AND
HIS SONGS

住在屏東恆春、家徒四壁、無親無故、孑然一身的民間藝人陳達，抱著月琴到處吟遊、即興彈唱、出口成歌，他說：「歌是從肚子裡翻出來的，要想，也沒人會教的。」

1977 年，在許常惠的引介下，高齡七十一歲的民間樂手陳達，來到了台北，基金會為他錄製了《陳達和他的歌》唱片，不只記錄了恆春的歌謠，也記錄了恆春的歷史與文化。

Born an orphan living a lone, sparse life in Hengchun, Pingtung, Chen Da embarked on his folk singer journey with just a yueqin (moon guitar) in hand, wandering and singing as music and lyrics came into his mind– or as he put it, his belly: "No one taught me how to write songs, songs just sprang out from my belly."

With the help of Hsu Tsanghouei, then 71-year-old Chen Da connected with the Hong Foundation and came to Taipei to record his first album *Chen Da and His Songs*, putting on record not just the sounds, but the history and culture of his hometown Hengchun.

贊助雲門舞集原創音樂
SUPPORTING ORIGINAL MUSIC BY CLOUD GATE DANCE THEATRE

1978 年 12 月 16 日，美國宣布與台灣斷交，當晚雲門舞作《薪傳》在嘉義首演，低迷哀傷的氣氛籠罩現場。陳達〈思想起〉滄桑的歌聲訴盡先民來台的辛酸，讓所有人動容。因為唱片出版，因為雲門舞集的《薪傳》演出，人們的內心因歌聲深深觸動，更加認同台灣這塊土地了。

基金會自 1974 年開始贊助雲門舞集，支持臺灣音樂家譜曲與錄音製作，「用自己的音樂，跳自己的舞」。計有賴德和的《白蛇傳》、許博允的《哪吒》、馬水龍的《燭》、史惟亮的《小鼓手》，馬水龍的《冥路》、賴德和《孔雀東南飛》、溫隆信《看海的日子》、戴洪軒《過客》，以及李泰祥的《吳鳳》與《射日》等。

1970 年代，洪建全基金會支持一流的藝術家，以雲門舞集作為一個起點，也是此後洪建全基金會展開以「文化贊助來播種」的開端。

On December 26, 1978, the United States broke off diplomatic ties with Taiwan; on the same evening, Cloud Gate Dance Theatre debuted its latest production *Legacy* in Chiayi. It was a day where clouds of despair and sadness loomed large over the audience, and thus everyone was deeply moved by Chen Da's weathered voice as he sang the hardships of Taiwanese ancestors when they first stepped foot on the island in the song *Thinking Back (Si Xiang Qi)*. The release of Chen's album and the performance of *Legacy* really galvanized the emotions of the Taiwanese people at that time, stirring in them the profound sense of belonging to the land they live on, and to their country.

Since 1974, the Hong Foundation had supported Cloud Gate Dance Theatre by sponsoring the composing, recording and production of original songs by Taiwanese music artists, rooted in the belief that we should "sing our own songs, and dance our own dances." The Hong Foundation funded 14 productions in total, including: *The Tale of the White Serpent* by Lai Deho, *No Cha* by Hsu Poyun, *Candles* by Ma Shuilong, *The Little Drummer* by Shih Weiliang, *Underworld* by Ma Shuilong, *Peacocks Fly East-Southern Bound* by Lai Deho, *The Day We Go to See the Sea* by David Wen Loonghsing, *Passerby* by Tai Hunghsuan, and *Wu Fong, Shooting the Sun* by Lee Taihsiang.

Supporting first-class local artists in the 1970s, starting with Cloud Gate Dance Theatre, the foundation endeavor to preserve and cultivate cultural qualities that are uniquely Taiwan- by "sowing the seeds of culture."

右:《薪傳》和《哪吒》海報 雲門舞集提供
左:《白蛇傳》劉振祥攝影／雲門舞集提供
Right: Cloud Gate Dance Theatre performance
posters of *Legacy* (top) and *No Cha* (bottom) (photo
credits: Cloud Gate Dance Theatre of Taiwan)
Left: *Tale of the White Serpent* (photographer: Liu
Chenhsiang; photo credit: Cloud Gate Dance Theatre of Taiwan)

因為《書評書目》的出版在文化圈成為盛事，簡靜惠也因為喜歡閱讀、認識許多文壇上知名的作家文人。70 年代，在那個等同「台北大半個文壇」的林海音家的客廳裡，許多與基金會有深厚淵源的作家都曾齊聚於此。

左起：隱地、殷張蘭熙、林懷民、簡靜惠、黃春明 林海音攝影

The publication of *Shu Ping Shu Mu Review of Books and Bibliography* was greatly lauded in the literary circle, and being a bookworm herself, Celia got acquainted with many renowned writers and scholars. Back in the 70's, nearly all of literary society in Taipei would often gather in Lin Haiyin's living room, including many artists and writers who had close ties with the Hong Foundation.

From Left to right: Yin Ti, Nancy Ing, Lin Hwaimin, Celia Hong Chien Chinghui, and Hwang Chunming. (photographer: Lin Haiyin)

文化人遊山玩水。有鄭淑敏、
樊曼儂、吳靜吉、薇薇夫人、
簡靜惠、謝春德、許雅婷、
許博允等人。
Friends from literary and culture
circles relaxing on an outing in
nature, including Cheng Shumin,
Fan Mannong, Wu Jingjyi, Madame
Weiwei, Celia Hong Chien Chinghui,
Hsieh Chunte, Hsu Yating, and Hsu
Poyun

自 1975 年 9 月，視聽圖書館在台北南京東路開幕之後，為使音樂文化與兒童教育能讓更多人受惠，即擴大服務地區，1979 成立高雄分館，1981 成立台中分館，北中南的市民皆能享用。而基金會的各類出版品如書與唱片，也在館中陳列，供會員借閱或購買。

Since the opening of its first premises on Nanjing East Road in Taipei in September 1975, the Hong Foundation Audiovisual Library sought ways to extend its reach so that more people could benefit from music, culture and children's education. Branches in Kaohsiung and Taichung opened in 1979 and 1981 respectively, giving access to those who lived in northern, central and southern Taiwan. Publications, books and records on display in the branches were available to library members to borrow or purchase.

洪建全兒童文學
創作獎
1974–1992

THE HONG FOUNDATION
AWARD FOR CHILDREN'S
LITERATURE

為了讓兒童們有更好的讀物，為了提高國內兒童讀物的水準，為了培養我們自己的兒童文學家。於是在作家簡宛的提議下，洪建全基金會創辦了「兒童文學創作獎」，鼓勵本土作家為下一代創作，讓台灣的孩子讀自己的故事，而不再是外國翻譯的故事。

The Hong Foundation advocated quality reading for children, and endeavored to improve the content quality of children's literature and to nurture more home grown writers. Following the advice of writer Jane Shih, the foundation established the Hong Foundation Award for Children's Literature, encouraging Taiwanese writers to create stories for the next generation so that their children could read stories about their own land and culture, rather than stories translated from other languages.

簡靜惠向公公洪建全說，台灣的小孩很可憐，都沒有台灣自己的故事，長大後連自己的文化也都不清楚，所以創辦兒童文學獎就是要鼓勵別人「寫故事給你孫子看」，疼愛孫子的洪建全一聽，就懂了。因為他深信兒童是明日的希望，所以願意鼓勵本土的作家一起為兒童寫故事。

Celia Hong Chien told her father-in-law Hong Chienchuan that it's sad that Taiwanese children have no stories of Taiwan that they could listen to, and very little means to get to know the culture in which they live. The purpose of the Hong Foundation Award for Children's Literature was to encourage more people to "write stories for our grandchildren." Being the loving grandfather that he was, Hong Chienchuan completely understood this and was willing to support the initiative on children's literature, as it was also his belief that children are our hope for a better tomorrow.

劉宗銘提供 (photo credit: Liou Izongming)

1974 年，創辦洪建全兒童文學創作獎，是為了鼓勵兒童文學的創作風氣，隔年，視聽圖書館設立之後，所舉辦的各種活動則是希望能培養兒童從小閱讀文學、欣賞藝術的能力和品味。

簡靜惠的兒子洪裕鈞（左）與女兒洪于倫（右）從小也參加基金會舉辦的各項活動。圖為正在參加繪畫課。圖片皆為劉宗銘提供

The Hong Foundation Award for Children's Literature was established in 1974 to incentivize the production of more works on children's literature in Taiwan. The year after, following the opening of the Hong Foundation Audiovisual Library, series of programs were organized to promote reading and to cultivate art appreciation from a young age.

Royce YC Hong (left) and Jenni Hong (right), children of Celia Hong, at a drawing class. They've participated in many of the foundation's programs since they were little. (photo credits: Liou Tzongming)

孩子們讀著
基金會出版的書
Children perusing
books published by
the foundation at the
foundation

1974 年 4 月，第一屆洪建全兒童文學創作獎正式公開徵稿。

基金會對兒童文學的創作扮演著參與者、激勵者、支持者的角色，對於評審完全支持與信任，除了提供經費和人力的協助之外，不預設立場，不介入評審意見。基金會也會出版所有得獎作品，對於很多有才情卻無力負擔出版的創作者而言，除了得獎榮耀之外，能與讀者接軌的舞台是更為實際的。

第一屆評審委員召集人是知名作家，也是學者洪炎秋先生。委員共有十二位：林海音、林良、林鍾隆、琦君、潘人木、華霞菱、華景彊、蓉子、馬景賢、鄭明進、趙國宗、曹俊彥等，可以說是一時俊傑，國內兒童文學的權威。

In April 1974, the first Hong Foundation Award for Children's Literature launched its open call for submission.

The foundation participated in, encouraged and supported the production of children's literature, giving judges full autonomy and trust, providing manpower and funding as they went through all the submissions, never questioning or intervening in their evaluations and decisions. The Hong Foundation would also published the works of the award winners, providing practical support for the talented writers who could not afford to publish their own works, and connected the award-winning authors with their readers.

With renowned author and scholar Hong Yenchiu as lead of the first jury, the panel of 12 judges were all respected figures in children's literature at that time: Lin Haiyin, Lin Liang, Lin Chunglong, Qi Jun, Pan Jenmu, Hua Xialing, Ching Hsiang, Wang Rongzi, Ma Chinghsien, Cheng Mingchin, Chao Kuotsung and Tsao Jenyen.

洪建全認為每年的頒獎活動都應盛大舉辦，才能吸引社會大眾的目光，重視兒童文學的發展。

基金會是以培養本土兒童文學作家為重要目標，透過創作人才的養成，提升兒童讀物的水準，不分省籍、意識形態，只要是生活在這塊土地的人都支持。

基金會出版的兒童文學作品屢獲金鼎獎肯定，對出版者與作家都是最大的鼓勵。

Hong Chienchuan directed the annual award ceremony to be held exuberantly to attract public attention so that the cause of children's literature would be taken seriously.

The Award for Children's Literature's most important goal is to cultivate local writers of children's literature and, through that, improve the quality of children's books, and to support all writers, impartial to their political or ideological preferences.

The Hong Foundation's children's literature publications had won the Golden Tripod Award several times, a great encouragement to the publisher and the authors.

上：洪建全為第十一屆兒童文學頒獎典禮致詞
中：基金會特別設計給得獎者的獎牌
下：教育部贈與基金會的感謝狀
Top: Hong Chienchuan giving a speech at the 11th Hong Foundation Award for Children's Literature ceremony
Middle: Award trophies and plaques specially designed by the Hong Foundation
Bottom: Certificate of Appreciation awarded to the Hong Foundation by the Ministry of Education

上：作家李潼（賴西安）曾連續三年（1985－1987）得到「洪建全兒童文學創作獎」的少年小說獎的首獎。國立台灣文學館提供

下：1977 年，多本兒童文學創作獎榮獲金鼎獎「優良圖書類」獎項。

Top: Author Lai Hsian, aka Lee Tung, earned 1st place of the Hong Foundation Award for Children's Literature (young adult novel category) for three consecutive years (1985 - 1987).

(photo credits: National Museum of Taiwan Literature)

Bottom: Many of the books that received the Hong Foundation Award for Children's Literature also won the national Golden Tripod awards in the "good books" category in 1977.

有中華商場的記憶，
就有國際牌的記憶
A LEGACY SYNONYMOUS WITH THE MEMORY OF CHUNGHWA MARKET

1961 年，興建完成的八大棟與三層樓高的中華商場，是當時台灣最大的百貨商場，也是台北市的新地標。中華商場帶動城中區相連的西門町，呈現前所未有的繁盛榮景。超過一千家的攤商與店面，有販售音響和電器用品，有大江南北各省各地的美食，有音樂唱片行和最新的時髦的商品……可購物，可閒逛，還可成為孩子們的遊樂場。

伴隨著經濟發展，多年的繁華逐漸流逝，為配合都市更新、捷運板南線施工，1992 年 10 月 20 日進行拆遷，三十一年的中華商場，正式走入歷史。

作家白先勇的小說《孽子》(1983)、導演侯孝賢的電影《戀戀風塵》(1986)、屏風表演班創辦人李國修的舞台劇《京戲啟示錄》(1996)，和小說家吳明益的《天橋上的魔術師》(2011) 都曾以中華商場為時空背景來創造故事。

走在中華商場或是天橋上，抬頭一望，自 1964 年即豎立在此的國際牌霓虹燈塔是西門町繁華的見證，也讓國際牌的品牌形象深入人心。相信有中華商場的記憶，就會有國際牌的記憶。

The newly-constructed, eight three-stories buildings that made up Chunghwa Market was the biggest shopping center in Taiwan in 1961. It was the new landmark for the city of Taipei, bringing never seen before development to the neighboring Ximending and the adjacent Taipei Main Station area– over 1,000 street stalls and storefronts, selling all kinds of goods: stereos, home appliances, gourmet food, music records and the latest fashions. It was "the" place to shop, to hang out and to party.

As the economy grew, so did the once-bustling hub start to ebb. To accommodate for urban renewal plans and the construction of the Taipei City Metro Blue Line, Chunghwa Market was demolished on October 20, 1992, ending its glorious reign of 31 years.

Chunghwa Market was the backdrop for Pai Hsienyung's novel *Crystal Boys* (1983), Hou Hsiaohsien's movie *Dust in the Wind* (1986), Ping Fong Acting Troupe's play *Apocalypse of Beijing Opera* (1996), and Wu Mingyi's novel *The Magician on the Skywalk* (2011).

The "Guojipai" (國際牌) and "National" brand neon sign that has stood here since 1964 and easily came into view with a lift of the head when in the area, bore testament to the then beating heart of Taipei- the Ximending area; its monumental letter "N" deeply embedded in the minds of those passing through the shopping mall or on the skywalk. If Chunghwa Market lives on in your memory, the "Guojipai" brand would live alongside it.the National brand would live alongside it.

上：中華商場　上頁圖皆為聯合報新聞圖片
下：中華商場還成了孩子們的臨時棒球場 (1989 年) 謝三泰攝影
Top: Chunghwa Market (photo credits: United Daily News)
Bottom: An empty street in front of Chunghwa Market made a great
spot for a game of baseball (1989). (photographer: Hsieh Santai)

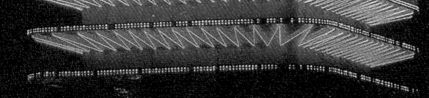

洪建全常常說：「若沒有洪游勉，就沒有國際牌。」
夫妻倆感情深厚，半世紀的攜手奮鬥，打造了家電品牌的龍頭地位。

Hong Chienchuan said this often: "The "Guojipai" (國際牌) brand would not exist if it weren't for Hong Youmian." The deep bond and companionship between husband and wife spanning over half a century made them industry leaders of their time.

基金會的好書
HONG FOUNDATION
PUBLISHING

洪建全基金會自 1972 年成立書評書目出版社至今，包括《書評書目》雜誌、兒童文學創作獎得獎作品的出版或專為孩童策畫出版的本土童書系列等，與 PHP 研究所合作出版的 PHP 叢書，以及各類自製策畫出版的本土作家如陳怡安、傅佩榮、林清玄等人的作品，一共出版將近八百本書，除了內容豐富多樣，亦曾獲得各式獎項。如 1977 年，兒童文學創作獎作品榮獲金鼎獎優良圖書類獎項；1979 年，《書評書目》榮獲金鼎獎雜誌類獎項；1985 年，榮獲金鼎獎頒贈「獎助出版事業及出版有功」；2007 年，榮獲金鼎三十給予「老字號金招牌」資優出版事業特別獎。

Since its establishment in 1972, the Hong Foundation Shu Ping Shu Mu Publishing, which later became Hong Foundation Publishing, has produced nearly 800 publications including the *Shu Ping Shu Mu Review of Books and Bibliography* magazine, award-winning works of the Hong Foundation Children's Literature Awards, Taiwanese children's literary collections, the jointly published PHP Institute book collection, and assorted individual publications of authors like Chen Yian, Fu Peijung and Lin Chinghsuan and many others.

The publishing catalog carries rich and diverse titles that had received numerous awards in various categories at the Golden Tripod Awards over the years. Multiple publications that had won the Hong Foundation Award for Children's Literature also received the national Outstanding Book Award in 1977; *Shu Ping Shu Mu* won the award in the magazine category in 1979; and the foundation received an Award of Merit for Publishing Fellowship and a special award for Outstanding Seasoned Publisher in 1985 and 2007, respectively.

1978 年，洪建全先生由行政院副院長徐慶鐘手中接下金鼎獎獎座。
Hong Chienchuan accepting a 1978 Golden Tripod Award from then-Vice Premier Hsu Chingchung.

文經學苑 1984-1995
THE CULTURE FOR BUSINESS ACADEMY

上：1986 年，洪建全、洪敏隆、簡靜惠、陳怡安等人拜訪日本 PHP 研究所。
下：1986 年，豐富人生系列講座的海報
Top: Hong Chienchuan, Hong Minlong, Celia Hong Chien Chinghui, Chen Yian, and others visiting the PHP Institute in Japan, 1986.
Bottom: A poster for the Life Enrichment Seminar Series, 1986

時任台灣松下電器公司董事長的洪敏隆於 1983 年間，參加日本 PHP 研究所的企業經營者研討會之後，他深受啟發，認為台灣也應該有以經營哲學及擴展現代胸襟的課程及研討會，因為企業人需要的不僅是企業經營的知識及方法，還應該有「人文」，也就是對「人」的認識及關懷。於是他將「文化」與「經濟」結合，於 1984 年 9 月成立「文經學苑」，由洪敏隆擔任苑長。

文經學苑希望藉由舉辦各式演講座談、研討會、研習營等，提倡領導者的人文素養。曾舉辦「企業與社會發展」座談會，邀請歷史學家許倬雲教授與陳怡安博士主講。時任聯電總經理的曹興誠也曾參加此活動（請見右頁圖）。

陳怡安帶所領的「激勵生命方法研習營」強調以人為中心、尊重生命；以傾聽接受、平等回應，讓參與者能統整或重新解讀個人的生命經歷，激發生命潛能與善良。也推出「豐富人生系列講座」，以人文精神為主軸，討論當代人的工作、生活與人生價值。

Hong Minlong (M.L.), then Chairman of Panasonic Taiwan, found himself deeply inspired after attending the Japanese PHP Institute's Management Seminar in 1983. He believed that Taiwan should also hold courses and seminars that focus on business philosophy and the expansion of modern minds; for business leaders need to know not only the know how and methods of business management but also the humanities as well– that is, the understanding and empathy for people. Thus, he combined "culture" and "business" to establish the Culture For Business Academy in September 1984, with himself as head of the Academy.

The Culture For Business Academy advocated humanistic qualities in leaders through various lectures, seminars and workshops, such as the Corporate and Social Development Symposium with historians Professor Hsu Choyun and Dr. Chen Yian as speakers. Then President of United Microelectronics Corporation (UMC) Robert Tsao was one of the many business leaders who attended the symposium (below).

The Life Workshops, led by Dr. Chen Yian, emphasized a people-centric approach and respect for life. By listening, accepting, and responding to others as equals, the workshop gave participants the opportunity to assess and reinterpret personal experiences, to spark their compassion and life potential. The Life Enrichment Seminar Series was another program that focused on contemporary work, life, and the value of life.

敏隆講堂
MINLONG FORUM

右圖：2013 年 4 月，鄭清茂教授在敏隆講堂講述日本文學。
左下：簡靜惠創辦敏隆講堂的初衷是希望讓懷抱多元關懷與專長的
講師來授課，吸引各階層人士、不分貧富貴賤都能來聽課，讓知識普
及。自左至右：鄭治桂寫春聯，張大春空中敏隆講堂的小說課，劉岠
渭講音樂，陳芳明談台灣文學史，楊照的歷史課，傅佩榮的哲學課。

Top right: A class by Cheng Chingmao on Japanese literature in session at
Minlong Forum April 2013
Bottom left: Celia Hong Chien Chinghui's original intention for Minlong Forum
was to allow lecturers with diverse expertise to teach, to attract people from
all walks of life, regardless of stature or wealth, to attend the lectures and to
popularize knowledge. Minlong Forum Forum lecturers (left to right): Cheng
Chihkuei writing spring couplets, Chang Tachuen (Minlong Forum: literature
on Air), Liu Chuwey on music, Chen Fangming on history of Taiwanese
literature, Yang Chao on history and Fu Peijung on philosophy.

素直友會
PHP SUNAO COMMUNITY

上：書法藝術家董陽孜老師為「素直」題字
下：素直友會的讀書會朋友可以自在讀書、旅行、看戲、也可徜徉在大自然裡。
Top: Calligrapher Grace Tong Yangtzu's Chinese characters of sunao for the foundation
Bottom: PHP Sunao Community book club members read, travel, watch movies, as well as enjoying nature together.

1986 年，洪建全帶著洪敏隆、簡靜惠等人訪問日本 PHP 研究所、真真庵等地之後，簡靜惠與洪敏隆對素直精神深有體會，也親見素直精神在個人、家庭、職場、學校與社區所發揮的影響力，於是在 1987 年正式在台灣成立「台灣 PHP 素直友會」。

簡靜惠說，素直友會的成立與參與，是她個人生活型態的表徵，得以用「素直心」與朋友歡聚，讀書、運動、培訓讀書種籽。在享受生活的同時，也散播讀書學習的種籽，可說是「修己助人」的自我實踐。

2018 年秋天，簡靜惠與已出任台灣松下電器董事長的兒子洪裕鈞及公司主管一起造訪真真庵，當年是與公公、丈夫，如今是與兒子重遊舊地（請見上圖）。

In 1986, Hong Chienchuan brought along Hong Minlong, Celia Hong and others to visit the PHP Research Institute and the venerated Shinshinan in Japan. During their stay, the spirit of *sunao* (a Japanese word meaning open-minded, honest, and good-natured) resonated deeply with Minlong and Celia, where they also personally witnessed the positive effect *sunao* had on individuals, families, workplaces, schools and communities. As a result, they were inspired to formally establish the Taiwan PHP Sunao Community in Taiwan upon their return.

Celia Hong views the establishment and her participation in the PHP Sunao Community as representative of her personal lifestyle. She embraces the *sunao* spirit in gathering with friends to read, exercise and her cultivation of numerous book club leaders. Being able to enjoy life while simultaneously sowing the seeds of reading and learning is a realization of the principle "In helping others, you help yourself."

In autumn of 2018, Celia Hong visited Shinshinan once more, this time accompanied by her son Royce YC Hong, who had already undertaken the role of Chairman of Panasonic Taiwan, and his company executives. The garden she once enjoyed with her father-in-law and husband, she has now revisited with her son (above).

台大
洪建全紀念廳
HONG CHIENCHUAN
MEMORIAL HALL

洪家第三代長孫媳張淑征建築師及十一事務所建築團隊設計的「台大洪建全先生紀念廳」，是以洪建全先生的肖像，及其事業與志業的代表地標：國際牌霓虹燈塔照亮的街景與洪建全基金會原址結合的圖像，融入在空間中，以橡木實木支柱構成的嵌入式壁畫中，透過橡木虛實律動與光影變化，彷彿聲波流動紋理，既懷念洪建全以修理收音機起家，同時也呈現他踏實創業的經營成就。

設置在台灣大學管理學院十樓的「洪建全先生紀念廳」各景(106-109頁)。李國民攝影

The Hong Chienchuan Memorial Hall in the business college of the National Taiwan University was designed by Hong Chienchuan's granddaughter-in-law Grace Cheung, an architect with her own practice XRANGE. Hong's portrait and the two streetscapes that captured his legacy– the images of the National neon billboard illuminating the streets and the original site of the Hong Foundation– were embedded within solid oak pillars as negative spaces; appearing amidst the rippled surface in-between the oak pillars with a strong interplay of light and shadow. The sound wave-like pattern not only referenced Hong's beginnings as a radio repairman but also symbolizes his substantial business achievements as well.

Various details of the Hong Chienchuan Memorial Hall on the 10th floor of National Taiwan University's College of Management, page 106-109. (photographer: Lee Kuomin)

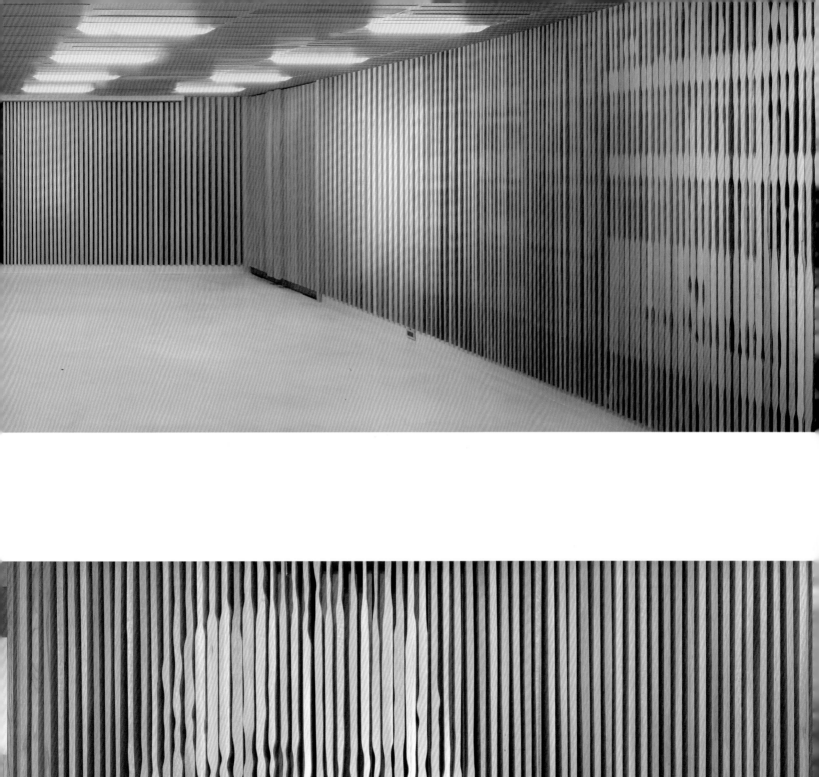
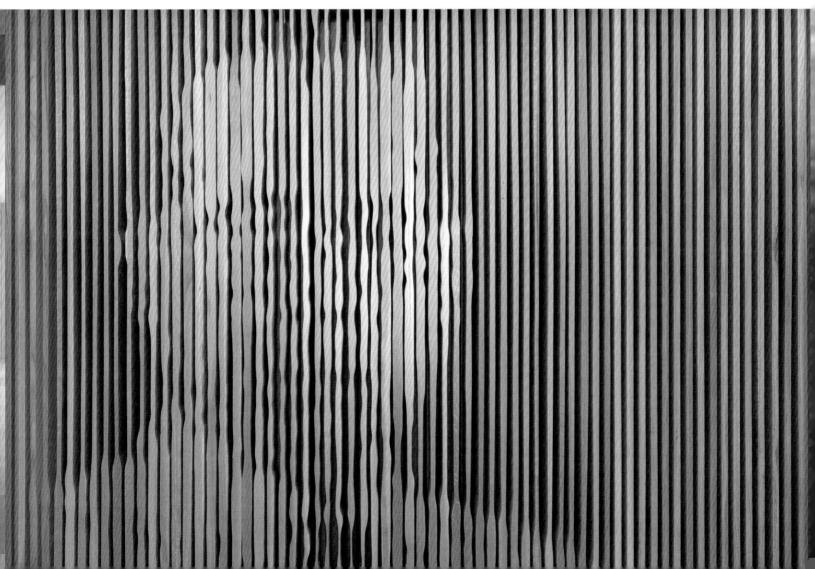

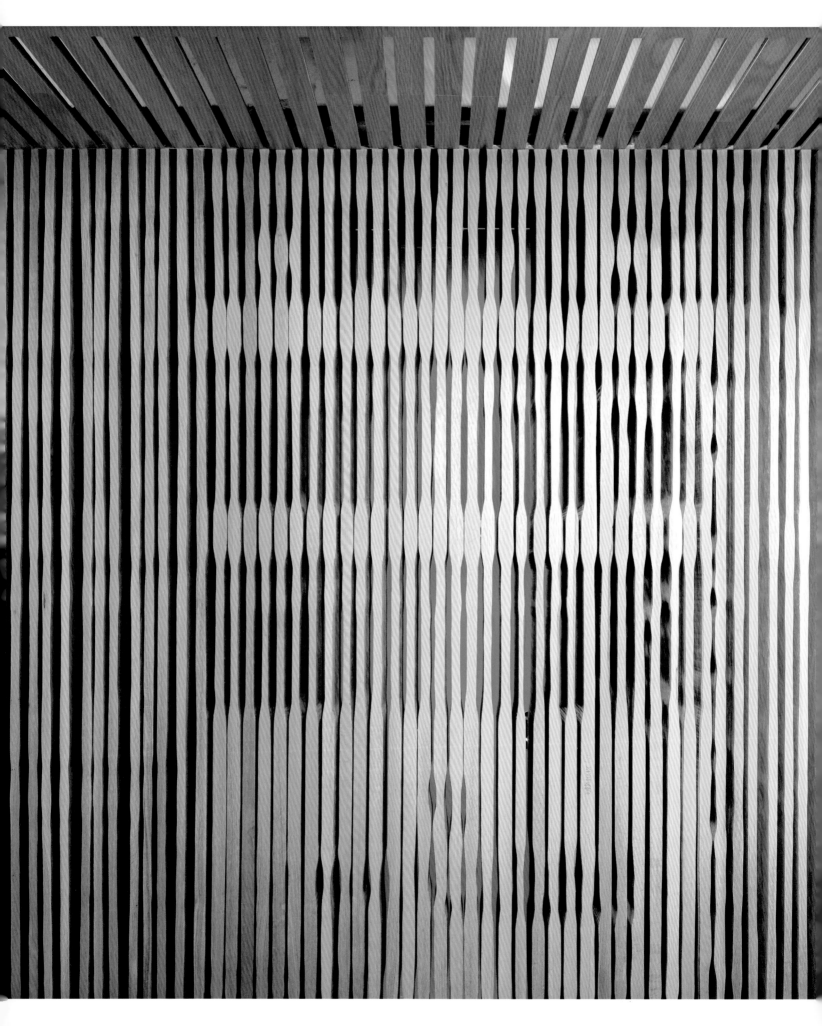

覓空間
MEME SPACE

2007 年，基金會的空間改修之後，代表著基金會將逐漸轉型。覓空間的設立，更呈現一種新意，擴大了原來文學、歷史、哲學、音樂與心靈探索的範圍，延展到更多當代多樣類型的文化和藝術，以鼓勵創意、跨領域研究與共同合作的形式。

覓空間同時具備多元功能，可舉辦藝術家作品、裝置藝術或新媒體等展覽。當敏隆講堂的講座聽眾過多時，也可延伸成為聽眾席。從敏隆講堂的中國古典元素轉移到金屬幾何的覓空間，呈現出基金會能將傳統與現代、古老與新穎融合為一。

After a renovation in 2007, the foundation gradually underwent its own transformation as well. The establishment of MEME Space represents the expansion of the foundation's long established scope of literature, history, philosophy, music and spiritual exploration into more contemporary and diverse forms of culture and art; with programs gradually started to motivate creativity and interdisciplinary collaborations and research.

As a multifunction space, it's a place for exhibitions, installation art or new media art. It is also the catchment area for Minlong Forum for when there are overflowing students for its classes. Shifting from the classical Chinese elements of Minlong Forum to the geometric, metallic MEME Space underscores the foundation's intention of blending seemingly polar opposites of old and new to create a new unity.

覓計畫
PROJECT SEEK

覓計畫是基金會文化播種與藝術實踐的平台，以創作者的角度出發，構築跨世代多元的文化生態，啟動不同尺度的贊助計畫來回應行進中的當代藝術。包括「問問題計畫」是以提問式的策展方式，委託製作全新的藝術創作；「認養計畫」是支持贊助獨特且具有國際發展潛力的藝術家；「雨棚計畫」則是於每年徵選不限類型的藝術展演活動。

基金會將啟動下一個五十年計畫，鼓勵未來世代提出各種最新的想法和見解，期待建立一個有機的創作生態系統，持續為社會帶來嶄新的觀點。

Project Seek is Hong Foundation's platform for cultural transmission and artistic practice. Founded with creators in mind, it aims to construct a diverse, multi-generational ecosystem through sponsorship programs of varying scales to support ongoing contemporary art. Key programs include the Question Project, an annual commission for a new work of art; the Extension Project, a sponsorship for artists with global potential; and the Canopy Project, an annual open call for artistic entries of any genre in any format.

The Hong Foundation aims to launch into the next 50 years with programs to invigorate future generations to express their unprecedented ideas and fresh perspectives. Through this endeavor the foundation hopes to establish an organic creators ecosystem that will continue to introduce new and powerful insights to society.

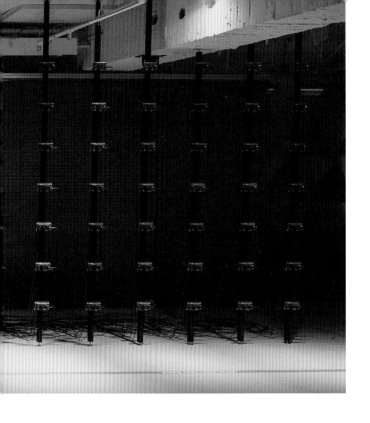

左上：問問題計畫 2019｜張永達個展—《Without Composing》
中：問問題計畫 2018｜李明學個展—《邊界》
右下：問問題計畫 2016｜張碩尹 × 鄭先喻—《棲息地》
Top left: Question Project 2019 | *Without Composing*, Chang Yungta
Middle: Question Project 2018 | *Boundary*, Lee Minghsueh Solo Exhibition
Bottom right: Question Project 2016 | *Second Life*, Chang Tingtong × Cheng Hsienyu

問問題計畫
The Question
Project

「問問題計畫」每年提出一個單純的問題,探討社會、文化與生命內涵。透過藝術家的新創作回應問題,挑戰當前既定觀點,啟發你我更多的提問。在「問問題計畫」中,藝術家以不同形式呈現所關注的議題,具公共性與教育性,吸引跨世代一起互動對話、參與體驗的方式來瞭解藝術家創作理念。

The Question Project poses one Question each year to explore ideas on society, culture, and existence. By commissioning one artist to react to the Question, the foundation hopes to spark participants' questions on the Question, so that they may infect others with other questions. Via the Question Project, artists present their concerns in diverse forms and mediums, a part of which is an education experience created for the general public. One of the mission of the Question Project is to promote cross-generational dialog through active engagement in the artists' creative processes.

雨棚計畫
The Canopy
Project

「雨棚計畫」是每年對外公開徵件，提供年輕藝術家和創作者舉辦個展或表演機會。鼓勵自由的藝術探索與更多實驗性的藝術創作，包含寫作、繪畫、雕塑、電影、動畫、數位藝術、新媒體裝置，以及戲劇表演等。

The Canopy Project is an annual open call for a solo exhibition or performance by young artists and creators, to promote artistic exploration of any genre in any format, and to foster experiment and play. Recent submissions had ranged from drawings, writing, painting, sculptures, film, animation, digital art, multimedia installations, performances to theatre.

左：黃翊《小螞蟻與機器人：遊牧咖啡館》，2020 年於國家戲劇院正式發表演出，張淑征擔任舞台裝置設計。
右上：雨棚計畫 2018 | 慶慶慶─《曾慶強個展》
右下：認養計畫 2017 | 石晉華─《行路一百公里》於香港巴塞爾藝術博覽會
Left: *Little Ant & Robot: A Nomad Café*, by Huang Yi. The performance premiered in 2020 at the National Theatre of Taiwan, with set installations designed by Vice Chairman Grace Cheung.
Top right: Canopy Project 2018 | *Rexy Tseng Solo Exhibition*, Rexy Tseng
Bottom right: Extension Project 2017 | *A 100 km Walk*, Shi Jinhua at Art Basel Hong Kong

銅鐘藝術賞是簡靜惠女士為紀念父親簡銅鐘因文學、藝術與電影養分豐富生命而設立，自2015年起，每年捐贈100萬元，支持傑出藝術家與作家們的創作成果。2015至2017年以推廣華文作家及其作品為主；2018至2021年贊助跨文化且具國際視野的當代藝術家。延續洪建全基金會的「播種」精神，由副董事長張淑征負責策劃，以文化創投的前瞻概念出發，基於對藝術家創作理念的信任，在概念階段即給予肯定，並支持其藝術的實踐。

「銅鐘經典講座」2015年至2017，分別邀請旅居加拿大華人作家張翎、香港作家陳冠中與中國大陸小說家畢飛宇陸續來台，於敏隆講堂舉辦民間講學，並擔任大學的駐校作家。

「銅鐘藝術賞」2018至2021年，在藝術家創作萌芽階段就給予贊助，如許家維的《熊貓、鹿、馬來貘與東印度公司》從數位時代物聯網智慧串聯看殖民時代以物易物的跨文化連結；鄭先喻的《同化者》探索人文與科技存在的焦慮和時代議題；林沛瑩的《Inter-(Being)》開啟病毒生態圈在人類及物種間文化結構。他們三位先後獲得此項殊榮。

上：2015年，加拿大華人作家張翎應邀來台參加首屆「銅鐘經典講座」，至花蓮東華大學擔任駐校作家，與學生們深度交流。
下：銅鐘經典講座三位作家在台出版的作品
右：第二屆銅鐘藝術賞｜2019 鄭先喻—《同化者》
Top: In 2015, Canadian Chinese writer Zhang Ling was invited to Taiwan to speak in the first Tung Chung Master Lecture Series lecture, and as the writer-in-residence at National Dong Hwa University, having in-depth exchanges with students.
Bottom: Taiwanese editions of works by the three Tung Chung Master Lecture Series lecturers
Right: Second Tung Chung Prize | *Assimilator*, Cheng Hsienyu, 2019

The Tung Chung Prize was established in 2015 by Celia Hong Chien Chinghui in honor of her father, Chien Tungchung, who enriched her life through literature, art and film. It is a one million NTD annual award to support an exceptional artist's creative output for a year. From 2015 to 2017, the prize was given to outstanding writers of Mandarin literature to promote their work; and from 2018 to 2021, to contemporary artists whose international perspective resonates throughout and beyond greater Mandarin cultures. Presided over by Hong Foundation Vice Chairman Grace Cheung, the Tung Chung Prize embodies the spirit of "cultural venture capital" by supporting creators and artists at the very early concept stage of creative work.

Through the Tung Chung Master Lecture Series held from 2015 to 2017, the foundation welcomed Chinese Canadian author Zhang Ling, Hong Kong-based author Chan Koonchung, and mainland Chinese author Bi Feiyu to Taiwan to hold public lectures in Minlong Forum, as well as serving as writers-in-residence within universities.

From 2018 to 2021, the Tung Chung Prize was awarded to Hsu Chiawei, Cheng Hsienyu, and Lin Peiying respectively. Hsu uses the analogy of Internet-of-Things (IoT) to reframe the colonial barter economy where multiple cultures crossed to astounding interwoven outcomes; Cheng explores the existential anxiety brought on by our dependence on technology; Lin examines the virus ecosystem through the cultural structure of humans and species.

銅鐘藝術賞
TUNG CHUNG PRIZE

HONG×PANASONIC
以科技驅動藝術
TECHNOLOGY
FOR ART

洪建全基金會秉持對文化播種的開創精神，五十年來支持贊助台灣藝術文化。覓計畫延續過去「洪建全視聽圖書館」對台灣藝文發展的支持，啟動不同形式的藝術贊助並引入最尖端的科技設備，回應藝術家的創作。2018 年起特別與台灣松下電器公司（Panasonic Taiwan）共同合作，提供贊助使用先進的多媒體設備器材，以科技結合藝術的方式，激發藝術家的創作動能。受贊助的藝術家以獨特視角創造出藝術的無限可能，陸續受到各界矚目。

如 2021 年，張碩尹、鄭先喻、廖銘和所創作的作品「台北機電人 2.0：訊息瘟疫」榮獲第 19 屆台新藝術獎的「視覺藝術獎」殊榮（請見右上圖），與入圍的《假使敘述是一場洪水— 劉玗個展》（請見上圖），都是基金會支持的藝術家。

基金會也安排藝術家與學者專家到台灣松下電器公司演講，是為：送人文到企業。許家維在台灣松下電器主講「拍攝者與被拍攝者之間的倫理問題— 以鐵甲元帥為例」（請見下圖）。

Upholding the foundation's pioneering spirit of "sowing the seeds of culture" and its 50 years support of Taiwan's art and culture, Project Seek continues the work of the Hong Foundation Audiovisual Library to provide cutting-edge technology and equipment to artists for their creations. Since 2018, the foundation has worked with Panasonic Taiwan to provide advanced multimedia equipment and professional tech support to artists, benefiting many artists who created infinite possibilities through their unique perspectives, which generated great public response through their work.

Beneficiaries of the Hong X Panasonic program shone at the 2021 19th Taishin Arts Award, *Taipei Robot Man 2.0: Infodemic* (top right), created by Chang Tingtong, Cheng Hsienyu, and Dino Mingho Liao, won the Visual Arts Award while Liu Yu's *If Narratives Become the Great Flood* (top) earned a coveted nomination.

For the last 10 years, the foundation has arranged for artists, scholars and culture experts to give lectures at the factories of Panasonic Taiwan as part of the Humanities For Business Program. Chia-Wei Hsu, recipient of the 2018 Tung Chung Prize, spoke on "The Ethics Between Photographers and Their Subjects: Taking the Marshal Tie Jia Project as an Example" at Panasonic Taiwan (bottom) in 2020.

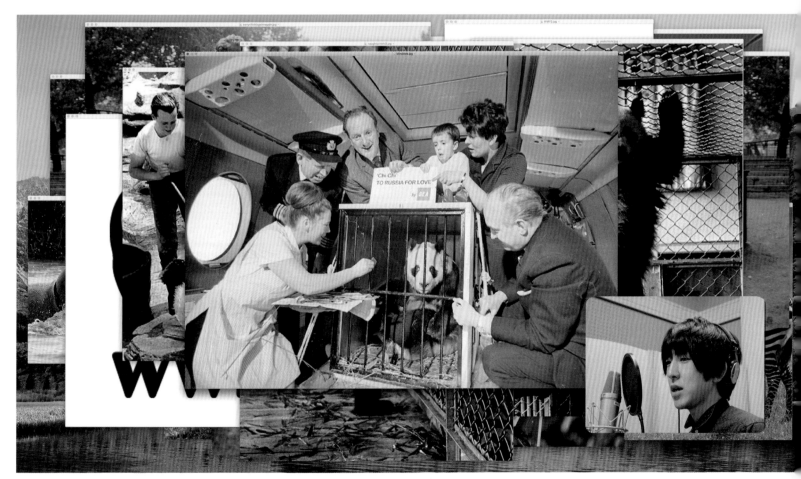

第一屆銅鐘藝術賞｜2018 許家維個展 —《熊貓、鹿、馬來貘與東印度公司》
First Tung Chung Prize | *Giant Panda, Deer, Malayan Tapir, and East India Company*, Hsu Chiawei, 2018

下一個 50 年 HAX
THE NEXT 50 YEARS- HAX

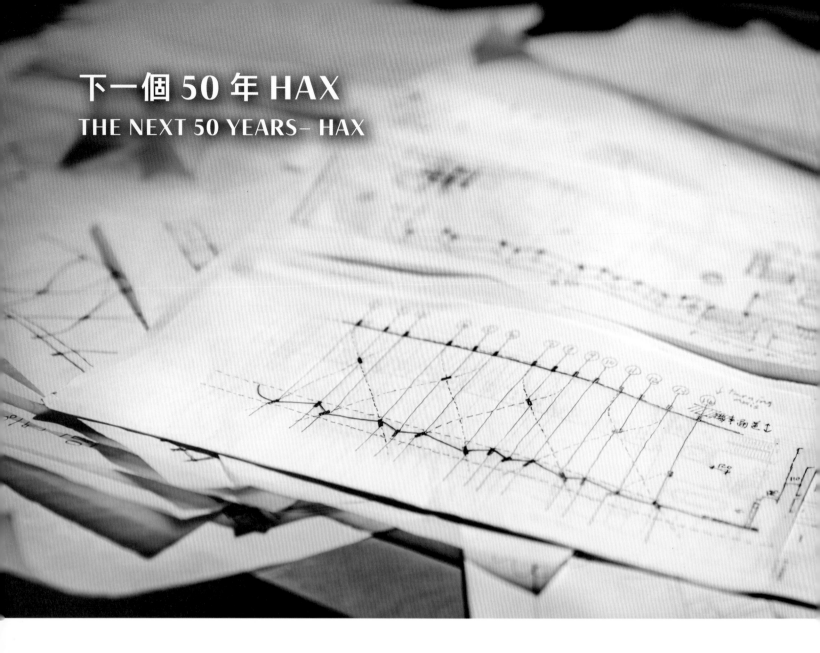

傳承洪建全先生收音機、電視機為文化載具的典範；洪建全基金會以「文化播種」的創新理念，五十年來耕耘出一片人文沃土；2021 年，基金會將啟動下一個五十年的發展引擎「HAX」。

HAX 計畫，是對於未來行創力的播種。HAX，是 Hong、Arts、Exchange 的組合。

HAX 的 X 意味不受限於任何形式的規範，是一種驅動能量，能夠連結各領域且彼此相輔相成；在展望未來的同時，也打造出一個屬於文化創作者的生態系統。

HAX 是永遠的現在進行式：將繼續推動人文教育、支持藝術家，以及持續在未來開發創造力。HAX 將本著播下文化種子的初衷和半個世紀以來，積累的能量與成果，以開放、熱情和謙遜的態度延續和發光。

Founder Hong Chienchuan saw radios and televisions as vehicles for cultural transmission, and for the past 50 years, the Hong Foundation has cultivated a fertile soil for humanistic traditions and ideas to continue to prosper and grow. 2021 and beyond, the Hong Foundation will launch its next 50-year initiative: HAX.

HAX is about investing in future creativity. HAX is the amalgamation of "Hong," "arts," and "exchange."

The "X" in HAX stands for "without any preset restrictions;" it is the driving energy that connects different fields of creativity; and while aiming towards the future, propels us to build an ecosystem of cultural creators.

HAX will be an on-going work in progress: the continual development of our work on art and humanities education, our continual support to artists and creators, and investments in future creativity. HAX will take our founding purpose of sowing the seeds of culture and the significant achievements we've accumulated over the past half century, carry them forward with open-mindedness, enthusiasm and humility.

左：承載著下一個 50 年，張淑征描繪 HAX 基地的設計手稿。

右上：2022 年，將在台北當代藝術館 MoCA 展出《轉接器 × 當代藝術》特展。 這是由洪建全基金會與台北當代藝術館共同合作的展覽計畫。左起台北當代藝術館駱麗貞館長、洪建全基金會副董事長張淑征、藝術家李明學、張碩尹、許家維、鄭先喻等人一起討論規劃。

右下：導演蔡弦剛為正在拍攝「洪建全基金會 50 週年」的紀錄片，採訪以《妹妹在哪裡？》得到第一屆兒童文學獎圖畫故事類首獎的劉宗銘老師。劉老師翻出多年前的資料與照片，訴說與基金會的故事。

Left: Grace Cheung's design sketches for HAX, the flagship headquarter building which will be the Hong Foundation's core for the next 50 years when built.

Top right: Headline exhibition *Adapter × Contemporary Art*, a collaboration between the Hong Foundation and the Museum of Contemporary Art Taipei (MoCA Taipei), opening 2022. From left, MoCA Director Lo Lichen, Hong Foundation Vice Chairman Grace Cheung, and artists Lee Minghsueh, Chang Tingtong, Hsu Chiawei, and Cheng Hsienyu on location at MOCA.

Bottom right: Film director Tsai Hsuankang interviewing author Liou Tzongming during the filming of the Hong Foundation's 50-year anniversary documentary. Liou, who won 1st Prize in the Illustrated Story Category of the first Hong Foundation Award for Children's Literature, showing the film crew old documents and photographs while sharing his story.

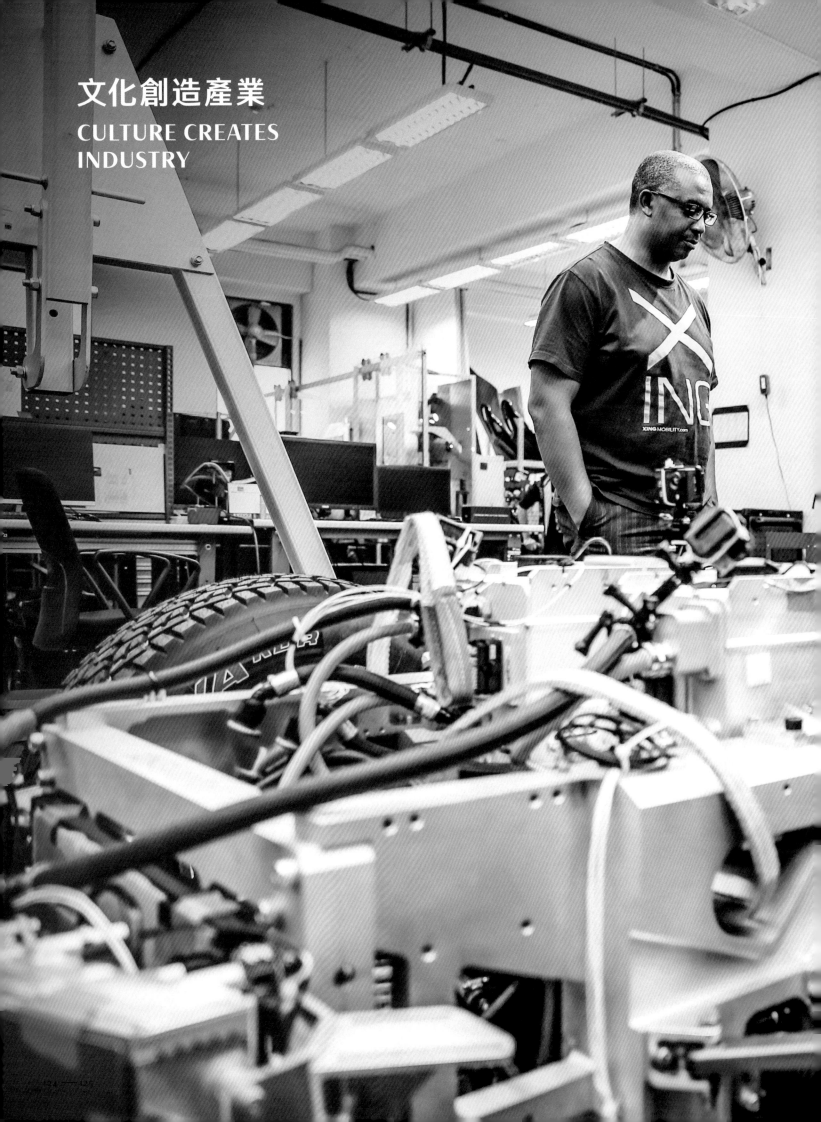

文化創造產業
CULTURE CREATES
INDUSTRY

洪建全基金會董事長洪裕鈞擁有跨領域背景，專業橫跨工業設計與科技創新。洪裕鈞身為 IPEVO 愛比科技創辦人暨董事長，旗下產品在美國 K-12 學校有超過 60% 滲透率；並與特斯拉前工程師一起創辦 XING Mobility 行競科技，打造全台第一輛電動超跑；目前亦擔任台灣松下電器董事長。

洪裕鈞承襲父親洪敏隆「雲與石—文化與經濟」的結合，更延展為「文化創造產業 Culture Creates Industry」，他認為人文藝術就是啟發未來產業的關鍵。他是跨領域的企業家，更是以設計思考為核心價值的創業家，將帶領基金會走向更多元、更前衛、更大膽、更創新、更令人耳目一新的未來。

Royce YC Hong, Chairman of the Hong Foundation, has a multidisciplinary background and his expertise spans the fields of industrial design and technology. He is also the Chairman and CEO of IPEVO, a maker of interactive teaching tools that are currently in use in over 60% of K-12 public schools in America. Additionally, he co-founded XING Mobility with a former Tesla engineer, successfully developing the first electric race car in Taiwan. Royce is also currently serving as the Chairman of Panasonic Taiwan.

Building upon his father Hong Minlong's thoughts encapsulated in his essay "Cloud and Stone: Culture and Industries", Royce advocates his "culture creates industry" philosophy– that humanities and the arts are critical in inspiring and driving future industries. A multifaceted business leader and an entrepreneur with a design thinking approach at his core, Royce will lead the Hong Foundation towards a more diverse, progressive, bolder, innovative, and exciting future.

前進未來
FUTURE FORWARD

洪建全基金會副董事長暨執行長的張淑征，生於馬來西亞、移民加拿大，是美國哥倫比亞大學建築碩士，曾任職於數個國際知名建築事務所，目前為十一事務所共同創辦人及主持建築師。其作品備受國際肯定，創作橫跨整體規劃、建築、產品與概念裝置等，概念思維及多元規模尺度在台灣獨樹一幟。張淑征從她的國際文化背景出發，將為基金會未來的五十年帶來多元化的新方向。

張淑征自 2007 年開始積極參與基金會事務，透過「覓計畫」，支持贊助台灣新銳藝術家。除了基金會原有的古典人文領域，當代新銳藝術也被納入視野之內。

透過建築，透過藝術，透過人文的跨領域學習……打破藩籬，打造美好的環境，傳承文化基因，是張淑征要給女兒和所有年輕的一代。

Grace Cheung, Vice Chairman and Executive Director of the Hong Foundation, was born in Malaysia and later immigrated to Canada in her teens. With a Master of Architecture from Columbia University in New York, she has gained international experience at several globally renowned firms before co-founding XRANGE; her works have received international recognition, with projects encompassing masterplans, architecture, landscape, products and installations, a diverse scope of projects that is one of a kind in Taiwan. With her culturally fluent background, Grace will bring forth new and diverse directions for the Hong Foundation's next 50 years.

Grace has been actively involved in the foundation since 2007, supporting and sponsoring emerging Taiwanese artists through Project Seek. Her introduction of Project Seek has expanded the foundation's fields of influence, beyond the previous quarter century's focus on classics and humanities into cutting-edge contemporary art.

Be it through architecture, art, or cross-disciplinary creative works– Grace hopes to break down barriers to build a culture engine to expand the Hong Foundation's legacy, to transmit the genetic codes of our cultural heritage to her daughter and to future generations.

圖為張淑征和女兒一同觀賞朱駿騰個展 — 八月十五
Grace Cheung and her daughter at Chu Chunteng's solo exhibition *Parallel*.

大事記
TIMELINE

1971–	成立洪建全教育文化基金會
	董事長—洪建全，執行長—簡靜惠

1972-1981	創辦《書評書目》雜誌，台灣第一本專業書評刊物
	發行人—洪敏隆，社長—簡靜惠，總編輯—柯青華 (隱地)

1972–	開始對外贊助
	設立空中學校獎金及貧病急危患者醫療基金
	鼓勵清寒學子繼續向學

1973–	成立書評書目雜誌附設出版社，後更名洪建全基金會出版社
	出版人文與經營管理書籍

1974-1992	成立洪建全兒童文學創作獎
	共舉辦 18 屆 (第 17~18 屆委由中華民國兒童文學學會辦理)
	贊助中華民國兒童文學學會 (1984 年成立)，並捐贈相關圖書與資料

1974–	開始藝文贊助
	贊助民族音樂調查、研究、保存與出版
	贊助蒐集與出版中國當代音樂、台灣校園民歌 (楊弦)
	長期贊助藝文團體：雲門舞集、廖瓊枝歌仔戲、優人神鼓等

1975-1989	成立洪建全視聽圖書館
	館長—林宜勝
	出版《國際視聽月刊》，刊登音樂相關訊息及基金會行事
	1976—1989：成立附設兒童閱覽室
	1991：捐贈館藏唱片與資料予國立臺北藝術大學音樂系

1977	兒童文學創作獎獲新聞局金鼎獎—優良圖書類
	《民族樂手—陳達和他的歌》獲首屆金鼎獎—唱片類
	簡靜惠因創辦《書評書目》雜誌等文化事業獲第十屆十大傑出女青年

The Hong Foundation established

Hong Chienchuan (C.C.), Chairman; Celia Hong Chien Chinghui, Executive Director

Publication of *Shu Ping Shu Mu Review of Books and Bibliography,* Taiwan's first professional book review magazine

Hong Minlong (M.L.), Publisher; Celia Hong Chien Chinghui, Director; Ko Chinghwa (aka Yin Ti), Editor-in-Chief

Charitable outreach programs launched

Established 'School on the Air' scholarship program & medical fund for critically ill patients in-need
Encouraged children of financially disadvantaged families to stay in school

Shu Ping Shu Mu Publishing founded (later renamed the Hong Foundation Publishing)

Publication of humanities and management-related books

The Hong Foundation Award for Children's Literature established

Ran for a total of 18 years (17th & 18th annual awards organized by Taiwan Society of Children's Literature)
Financially supported Taiwan Society of Children's Literature (est. 1984) along with donations of books and materials

Charitable support for art and culture begins

Sponsors surveys, research, conservation, and publishing work related to folk music
Sponsors the compilation and publishing of contemporary Chinese music and Taiwan contemporary folk songs (e.g. Yang Hsien)
Provides long-term support for art troupes & organizations: Cloud Gate Dance Theatre of Taiwan, Liao Chiung-Chih's Taiwanese Opera, and U-Theatre

The Hong Foundation Audiovisual Library opened

Katz Lynn, Head Librarian
Published *National AudioVisual Monthly,* a magazine about music and the Hong Foundation affairs.
1976 - 1989: Maintained a dedicated children's reading room
1991: Donated in-house collection of records and related materials to the Taipei National University of the Arts School of Music

The Hong Foundation Award for Children's Literature received a Golden Tripod Award (book category) from the Government Information Office
A Folk Musician: Chen Da and His Songs received Golden Tripod Award (record category)
Celia Hong Chien Chinghui honored at the 7th Ten Outstanding Young Women Awards for her creation of *Shu Ping Shu Mu Review of Books and Bibliography* magazine and other culture related work

| 1979 | 《書評書目》雜誌獲金鼎獎—雜誌類 |

1984-1995 成立文經學苑
苑長—洪敏隆
提倡領導者人文素養與舉辦人文藝術講座

1985 獲金鼎獎—獎助出版事業及出版有功

1986-1998 激勵生命方法研習營
陳怡安主持

1987- 成立台灣 PHP 素直友會
總會長—簡靜惠
推動讀書風氣與修己助人的素直精神
1988：與日本 PHP 研究所交流結盟
2002：與人間佛教讀書會結盟，於世界各地推廣閱讀風氣

1991-2020 成立洪敏隆先生人文紀念講座
引領時潮新論，喚起社會大眾對於人文價值的重視與思辯
前期由許倬雲與李亦園策劃，後期由簡靜惠統籌策劃

1993 洪敏隆家族捐出遺產，購置洪建全基金會會址：台北市羅斯福路二段 9 號 12 樓

1995- 啟用敏隆講堂
創辦人—簡靜惠
以人文為主軸，開辦文、史、哲、藝等課程透過系統性、長期與深入的學習方式，
帶動社會學習人文風氣。

2004- 送人文到企業
2004 至今：台灣松下電器公司
2011、2015：廈門建松電器公司

Celia Hong Chien Chinghui, Founder
Established a humanities lecture hall that offers courses in literature, history, philosophy and the ar
Promotes popular interest in the humanities through systematic, long-term, and in-depth lectures

Humanities For Business Program launched

2004 - present: Panasonic Taiwan
2011 & 2015: Panasonic Manufacturing Xiamen

2007–	**成立覓計畫 Project Seek**
	張淑征創辦、主持
	覓計畫 (Project Seek) 為建全基金會開創性的文化播種與藝術實踐的引擎，以創作者 (Creator) 尋覓創變基因的觀點出發，構築跨世代多元的文化生態 (Culture of Creation)，啟動不同尺度的贊助計畫來回應行進中的當代藝術。

2007–	**素直友會關愛計畫**
	於偏遠山區學校推動結合身心靈合一的學習
	贊助伊苞老師至南投親愛國小鼓樂教學

| 2007 | 獲金鼎三十「老字號金招牌」資優出版事業特別獎 |

| 2013– | **設洪建全先生紀念講座** |
| | 洪建全基金會、建弘文教基金會合辦 |

2015–	**設銅鐘經典講座／銅鐘藝術賞**
	為感念父親栽培養育之恩，簡靜惠董事長個人每年捐助一百萬元設立
	2015 — 2017：以文學為主—銅鐘經典講座
	2018 — 2020：以藝術為主—銅鐘藝術賞

2021–	**《書評書目》再現**
	網路版，贊助新匯流基金會
	數位資料庫，與聯合知識庫合作

2021–	**HAX 計畫 典範移轉**
	洪裕鈞、張淑征主導
	傳承洪建全先生將收音機、電視機視為「文化載具」的典範，「HAX 計畫」將是洪建全基金會下一個五十年的發展引擎。

Project Seek launched

Grace Cheung, Founder and Project Director
Project Seek is the Hong Foundation's platform for cultural transmission and artistic practice. Founded with creators in mind, the Project aims to construct a diverse, multi-generational ecosystem through sponsorship programs of varying scales to support ongoing contemporary art.

PHP Sunao Outreach Program launched

Promotes mind-body-spirit learning at schools in remote areas of Taiwan
Sponsors Dadelavan Ibau in teaching drum classes at Chin Ai Elementary School in Nantou County

Received special recognition award at the 30th Golden Tripod awards for long-running contributions to the publishing industry

Hong Chienchuan Memorial Lecture Series established

Co-organized by the Hong Foundation and NSFG Foundation

Tung Chung Master Lecture Series & Tung Chung Prize established

Funded by an annual NT$1 million donation made by Celia Hong Chien Chinghui in memory of her father
2015 - 2017: Literature- Tung Chung Master Lecture Series
2018 - 2020: Art- Tung Chung Prize

Reintroduction of *Shu Ping Shu Mu Review of Books and Bibliography*

Supported Hyper Convergence Foundation in publishing of digital version
Cooperated with UDN Data on digital database development

HAX Project: Shifting Paradigm

Royce YC Hong and Grace Cheung, Initiators
Continuing in founder Hong Chienchuan's view of radio and television as vehicles for cultural transmission, HAX is the engine driving the Hong Foundation forward through the next fifty years.

洪觀時代
洪建全基金會 50 年
TRANSFORMING VISIONS
HONG FOUNDATION 50 YEARS

總 編 輯	張淑征	Executive Editor	Grace Cheung
編輯顧問	曾文娟	Consulting Editor	Sophia Tseng
編輯小組	蔡依汝 邱惠儀 朱公望	Editing Team	Esther Tsai, Waverly Chui, Jerry Chu
美術設計	李思佳	Artistic Design	Gina Li
英文翻譯	米傑富 蘇珏于 陳怡如	English Translation	Jeffrey Ryan Miller, Su Chuehyu, Ada A. Chen

發 行 人	洪簡靜惠	Publisher	Celia Hong Chien Chinghui
出 版 者	財團法人洪建全教育文化基金會	Published by	The Hong Foundation
	地址：100420 台北市羅斯福路二段 9 號 12 樓		ADD: 12F, No.9, Sec. 2, Roosevelt Rd., Taipei City, 100420, Taiwan
	電話：(02)23965505		TEL: +886-2-23965505
	傳真：(02)23922009		FAX: +886-2-2392-0009
	https://hongfoundation.org.tw		https://hongfoundation.org.tw

印 刷 者	傑崴創意設計有限公司	Printer	Gateway Visual Creative Co.
定 價	新台幣 800 元 (精裝)	List Price	NT$800 (limited edition)

國家圖書館出版品預行編目 (CIP) 資料

洪觀時代：洪建全基金會 50 年 / -- 第 1
版 . -- 台北市：財團法人洪建全教育文化
基金會，2021.11
面 ；公分
ISBN 978-957-0351-25-5 (精裝)
1. 洪建全基金會
068.33 110015667

HONG
FOUNDATION
洪建全基金會

書號 HB0446
ISBN 978-957-0351-25-5
Printed in Taiwan